Hot Ice Cream

Inspiring Life Lessons from Our Children

By Matthew J. Goldberg

Dedication

Especially for Mom, Sara Passo Goldberg, and
Benny's maternal grandfather, Tan Jijun.

Contents

Acknowledgments

Although this is a relatively small book (I know; *relative to what?*), it was compiled and written over a long period of time. While I pondered whether or not to turn these words of everyday, ironic wisdom (mostly *authored* by my young son, Benny) into a book, I want to thank all those who inspired and encouraged me to do so.

Tan Xiaoqian, who many here know as Ruby Tan, my loving and ever-patient wife: You are an amazing mom, and a great wife. You deserved a co-author's credit, and more, but you deferred to me on this. As a classic understatement, there is no Benny without you, and we both love you dearly.

Benny's aunts (Tan Ling [Linda], Tan Jie and Lorre), along with his cousins, Rachelle, Aimee, Liora, Eliana, Zhu Anqi [Cathy] and Alexander: Thank you for all of your love and friendship.

And his uncles, my older brothers Dan and Josh, also merit a mention for their own friendship and love.

Some of the following anecdotes and words of wisdom have been shaped by various friends, teachers, coaches, teammates and playmates. I've used *aliases* to conceal most of their identities along the way, but please know that we are grateful. As a collective shout-out, Benny has enjoyed inspiring early school experiences at all of his stops to date, including Barclay

Early Childhood Center, Joyce Kilmer Elementary School, Congregation Mkor Shalom, and Hua Xia Chinese School. All are located in Cherry Hill, New Jersey.

Many of my own in-person and virtual friends have expressed to me how much they have enjoyed the anecdotes (that have come to be known as Benny-isms) that I have posted on Facebook the last couple years. I appreciate your supportive comments, and even those semi-obligatory "likes." Your encouragement to turn these anecdotes into a book is also very much appreciated.

Encouragement has also been received from various friends and colleagues I have come to know from my speaking circles, including those of the Voorhees Toastmasters Club (part of District 38, for all my "Toastie" friends out there), and the Emerging Speakers Bureau. Feedback, mostly in the form of laughs, smiles and appreciation, has helped to shape and improve this book and my various presentations that have gone just a little deeper.

This book has also benefitted from the terrific work and high professionalism of my cover designer, Jennifer Givner of Acapella Book Cover Design, and the interior formatting of Aubrey and Joel of Penoaks Publishing.

The last person I will acknowledge here should really be the first—Benny.

Benjamin Jun (Benny) Goldberg:

In many ways, my life truly began on July 24, 2008, which, not so coincidentally, was the day you were born. It took me a long time to become a dad, and you are a better, more fascinating and wiser son than I ever could have dreamed of.

I hope that these anecdotes—loosely but lovingly recollected as they are—somewhat capture your essence. I also hope that they will bring you some measure of the joy that you have provided us, and afford you an appreciation of how much Mommy and I love you.

With eternal and monumental love and gratitude,

Matthew J. Goldberg

aka "Daddy"

2/2015

Preface

This is a book that revolves around stories, so I'll start with one.

My son Benny is three years old—make that three-and-a-half—at the time. I'm driving him and a few other family members home from a party. It's a little after midnight, and all four passengers, cramped together in my little car, are asleep. Or, so I think.

No, we're not a family of party animals, but it was a family event that we couldn't, and didn't want to, pass up. And yes, it's a verifiable fact that Benny was, and is, a night owl.

Earlier that night, Benny was given an ice cream bar, and it melted all over his hands and clothes before he got to finish it. Evidently, it made quite an impression on him. Suddenly, I hear his voice as I'm crossing the bridge.

"Dadd-yyyyyyyyyyyyyy."

"Yes?" I reply, with what must have been a surprised tone.

"I like hot ice cream," my little wonder says.

"Why, Benny?"

"Because it doesn't melt."

Of course, I had no reply for this other than laughter, but I freely admit that my son's irrefutable logic made that late February drive home a whole lot warmer.

Within a few months of the *hot ice cream* incident, I decided that it would be fun to try to record (at least on a keyboard) some of Benny's great lines. While I didn't record all of them (that would be impossible, as he's quite prolific), I tried to capture many, and also share a few with friends and family in that newly time-honored tradition. I posted some of these anecdotes on Facebook.

Over time and with some very encouraging words from friends—real and virtual alike—I thought that a compilation of what my wife Ruby and I came to experience as *Benny-isms* would inspire an interesting book.

This idea helped me recall one of our favorite Benny-isms from when he was young. Okay, he's *still* young, but let's go back to when he was *really* young. Age two. And no, he wasn't a terrible two—just a highly active one who was full of surprises. Oh, and he never cared too much for going to sleep at a normal hour.

This one evening—very late evening as befits his nocturnal nature—he is playing on the kitchen floor while Ruby is washing dishes. On our kitchen floor is a plastic container filled with uncooked rice. Benny knows how to pop the lid off. From there, he loves to roll his cars and trains around the kernels. It's mostly harmless fun, but Ruby isn't a big fan of this game that we call "playing rice." Meanwhile, I'm crashed out on the couch and oblivious to the scene of rice kernels flying all around the room.

I hear my wife's slightly distressed voice. "Honey, can you wake up and keep an eye on Benny."

Half-awake, I blurt out. "Hey Benny, is everything okay?"

My little guy, without missing a beat, is his reassuring and proud self. *"Don't worry, Daddy, I'm playing rice!"*

As usual, I didn't have a good reply to this remark. Whether two years old, six years old (which he very recently turned, as I'm writing), or (I suspect) when he turns 18 years old, Benny always has, and always will have, a knack for getting in the last word. This isn't always easy for this writer and public speaker to accept, but I have made peace with this reality.

While compiling these Benny-isms and debating whether or not a book would be a good idea, several questions came to mind. Here are five of those internal questions, and how I've managed to answer them.

What is so important about these anecdotes?

Nothing. And everything. Neither one of the two little incidents I just shared was particularly momentous, yet somehow stories like these mean the world to us. Yes, the specific memories captured a distinct place and time for us, but there's something more that makes them really resonate with others. They give us that precious gift of looking at the world in a whole new way, borrowing a new set of eyes and a fresher, less jaded (and less filtered) mindset from which we can view the world.

Yes, but who will be able to relate to them? They (many of you) don't even know Benny.

Benny is quite unique, but so are your sons, daughters, nieces, nephews and grandchildren. Part of the joy of compiling and recording these moments is preserving some of these memories for those who have gotten to know Benny. But, there's much more to this little story.

As unique and irreplaceable as Benny is to us, you feel the same way about other children who mean the world to you. Perhaps, you even remember being the same age(s) as the boy that is depicted here. Hopefully, in reading and sharing these little nothing/everything moments, they will also stir your own precious little stories to the surface.

You're confusing me. Is Benny a brilliant young boy with a totally unique way of looking at the world, or a typical boy of his age?

Yes. He's a little bit, or maybe *a lotta bit*, of both. I am constantly amazed at how he puts thought and ideas together, and it's a joy—mostly—to see the word through his eyes. And yes, once again, I would say that he is somewhat typical in this regard.

Are all these incidents and quotes accurate?

Yes, as close as I could recall. I see no point in exaggerating or fabricating these stories. In fact, there is every reason **not** to do this.

What have you learned through these nothing/everything moments, and what could they teach us?

I think that this question gets to the "why" of this book, and the "why" of this book has evolved. It started as a way to memorialize some of those nothing/everything moments and to provide some laughs and smiles. And yes, this approach has been done before, sometimes with great success.

In the process of compiling these stories, I wanted to take this book just a little deeper, and still keep it breezy and light. I wanted, and want, to encourage my fellow dads (and also, the moms, uncles, aunts and grandparents——and even siblings) to cherish these moments and what we can learn from them. At the very least, we can re-learn the lesson that our children don't want, need or expect us to have all the answers. (In my case, that's a very good, and empowering thing!) They don't need our perfection, but they do need our connection, our presence and our involvement. That is the greatest gift we can offer, and it is a gift that returns even more to us.

Many of these moments either directly or upon reflection taught me a little something. Within this little book are 100-plus life lessons derived from these "Hot Ice Cream" moments. Some are rather silly and trivial, but some go just a little deeper to remind us of something that we can apply to everyday life. Since I don't pretend to have all the answers, you may derive still other little life lessons from these stories. And if you just want to enjoy these stories because they take you to a particular time and place within your life (present, past or future), that is your prerogative.

However you view these stories, thank you for picking up a copy of this book. I hope that reading it will encourage you to take the time to encourage, cherish and share your own *Hot Ice*

Cream moments. Of course, in my little household, we call these moments "Benny-isms". Here's just one more Benny-ism—for now.

Benny is just starting kindergarten. I ask him if his class has line leaders, like they did when he was in pre-school. Today is his fourth afternoon of "K."

"Kind of", he manages.

"What do you mean by kind of?"

"They don't call them that."

"What do they call them?"

"Nothing."

(Maybe, I'll get in the last word this time.) "Have you been a nothing this year?"

"No, I never get to be a nothing."

(Maybe not.)

"So, what do you do?"

"I just line up with all the other somethings."

Of course, there are so many of these *nothing* moments that I am about to share with you. Please enjoy all of these momentous *nothing* moments, and may they also remind you of your own little *everythings*.

Matthew J. Goldberg

February, 2015

Do you ever hear your inner voice asking you these two questions? Simultaneously. How did it take me so long to get here? How did I get here so soon? If so, you're not alone.

"Bao"
Age 1.5

Benny is an awesome blend of wonderful qualities, but I wouldn't call him a great or independent sleeper. Great talker? Yes. By age one or so, he was putting together words in both English and Chinese (Mandarin). One of his favorite Chinese words was "bao", which is a command to pick him up.

Sleep? Well, I've always joked that Benny came out of the factory on Hawaii Time, and we never acclimated him to Eastern Time. He stays up verrry late.

And so it was one night, or perhaps very early morning, that Ruby and I were ready to go to sleep, having just gotten Benny to sleep in his crib across the hall. All was quiet, life was good, and we all but popped champagne corks in bed. Our heads just started to rest on our pillows when we suddenly heard, "Bao. Bao, Mama. Bao."

Never celebrate your triumphs prematurely.

Blueberry Festival
Almost 2

On a very hot weekend afternoon, we drive to a blueberry festival in the area that features all kinds of blueberry products, a petting zoo, pony rides and one main tent set up for entertainment.

Benny hears some kind of music from the main tent and disappears into a big crowd to be where the action is. (Mind you, this is the same kid who at this stage gets nervous if we aren't in the very same room of our not-exactly-palatial house.)

He makes it to the apron of the stage where the featured act is a troupe of Irish dancers ranging in age from about 5 to 16. As they're dancing, Benny is turning to the crowd to lead them in applause, practically stealing the show in the process.

Near the end of the show, the group's instructor brings up volunteers, and quickly snatches Benny—who hardly needs his arm to be twisted. He's still in good form on stage—and certainly none of this good form and apparent talent came from me or Ruby.

He is one of the first to walk off the stage and waits around to high-five each of the girls as they step down.

Bilingual Benny
Just Turned 2

Benny is talking to Ruby's Mom (his *waipo*), who only knows a few words of English. Unfortunately, I only know a few words of Mandarin. At a very early age, Benny has figured this out.

Waipo says something, and then my boy looks at me and translates it, before replying to her. He must be thinking *"This is for you, dummy"* before doing so, but I am grateful that he doesn't verbalize this.

As such, it's a beautiful thing, even if I am unimpressed with my own fleeting, futile attempts to be bilingual. Like him.

You may suspect that your son or daughter is smarter than you. Don't worry; your suspicion is probably on solid ground.

Playing Rice
Age 2

On our kitchen floor is a plastic container filled with uncooked rice. At an early age, Benny learned how to pop the lid off. Once the lid is unhinged, he loves to roll his cars and trains around. It's mostly good, harmless fun, but Ruby isn't a big fan of this game—we call it *playing rice*—and his spilling kernels all over the floor.

One evening, I'm resting on the couch, Ruby's washing dishes and Benny's doing his thing.

Ruby: Honey, can you wake up and keep an eye on Benny?

Matt (barely awake): Hey Benny, is everything okay?

Benny: (with great pride) Don't worry, Daddy, I'm playing rice!

One person's reassurance is (sometimes) another's cause for concern.

Ducking the Questions
Age 2.5

On the Jewish holiday of Passover, there is a special meal and service called the *Seder* (many observe it for the first two nights of the holiday), where one of the traditions is that the youngest child present recites *The Four Questions*. A lot of kids may start to memorize *The* 4 Questions—which are recited in Hebrew—at age four or so.

Benny and I had practiced them on a few occasions—only—and we wanted to see what he would be able to do, being delighted at whatever he would perform. When it comes time to do it at our Seder, he becomes very shy, and there being no other kids present, I end up chanting them in an obligatory way.

About an hour later during the dinner, Benny suddenly says, "Do you want to hear me do The Four Questions like a duck?" *Sure*, I reply. He then proceeds to do the first line or two, giving it his best Donald Duck impersonation: *"Ma nishtana, ha-laila ha-ze..."*

Our children are not trained seals: Don't expect them to perform on command.

Nothing
Almost 3

This may be a "you had to be there" moment, and I'll try to take you there.

Ruby and I are with Benny at a local park, and he is playing with a slightly older boy. I think his name is Steven but when they made introductions, the boy says, "My name's Nothing."

They play together for a little while longer; I can't remember Benny calling him by (either) name the whole time. Steven has to go and says, "Bye, Benny."

Benny replies: It was nice to play with you, Nothing.

Too Much Commercionals
Age 3

Benny certainly loves to watch television. One day, I turn it off, and anticipate his reaction.

Matt: Benny, you've been watching too much TV.

Benny: I don't watch too much TV; I watch too much *commercionals*.

When correcting others, always be specific.

Sideways
Age 3

Benny's playing with another boy at the playground nearby our house. They're sitting down on a little bench that is underneath one of the bridges that leads to a slide. The other boy, named *Karl*—around the same age, maybe a month older—starts talking:

Karl: Let's watch TV.

Benny: Yeah, we're watching TV.

Matt: What are you guys watching?

K: We're watching a movie.

M: What movie?

K: Winnie the Pooh

B: (pretends to pick up the remote control). I want to watch *Sideways.*

Your children pay attention to everything you say, do and watch.

Hi, Dally
Age 3

Pardon the boast, but my three-year-old has a huge vocabulary for his age in two languages, and has never stumbled over words like Pachycephalosaurus. However, he has this lazy "L" thing—mostly with D's and T's—that causes him to call me "Dally."

My favorite is when he plays or tells a little joke, and then says, "I'm just *killing* you." It does kill me—every time, and in all the right ways.

Three Little Toastmasters
Age 3

I had been practicing my speech a few times at home for a Toastmasters humorous speech competition. I adapted the classic story of The Three Little Pigs and the Big Bad Wolf (one of Benny's very favorite tales) and titled it something like *The Three Little Piggie Toastmasters and The Big Bad Speech Evaluator.*

Both Benny and Ruby had listened to me nervously go through it a few times, while trying to keep me within the allotted time frame. I had won my club's speech competition with it, and despite expecting to win the next round as well, finished as the runner-up.

I return home slightly dejected, but then receive a great, unscripted surprise. While in the bathtub, Benny is reciting about half of my speech.

Maybe, we should have changed places.

The best prizes are often the ones we don't actively pursue. Or, if you prefer: The best prizes are often surprises.

Hot Ice Cream
Age 3

We're driving home very late at night from a party at our cousin's house. Our car is full, I'm driving, and everyone else is asleep. Or, so I think.

At the party, Benny was given an ice cream bar which melted all over his hands and clothes before he was able to finish it. Evidently, it made quite an impression on him. It's very quiet, until...

Benny: Daddy.

Matt: Yes?

B: I like hot ice cream.

M: Why, Benny?

B: Because it doesn't melt.

Often, the best solutions are close at hand, and sometimes right on our hands and clothing.

Leaving
Age 3.5

Tonight, with Ruby away, I needed to bring Benny to my Toastmasters meeting—which lasts almost two hours, all-told. It was a pretty good meeting, and I included him (speaking in front of the group) when I could. On the way home, I ask him, "What was your favorite part of the meeting?"

With perfect timing, and absolutely no prompting, he replies, "Leaving."

We don't all share the same preferences.

I'm Wearing You In
Age 3.5

One late night, I'm trying everything in my power—reading, playing, more reading and more playing—to get Benny to go to sleep, but he's wired and I'm simply tired.

Matt (exasperated): C'mon, Benny, you're wearing me out.

Benny: You're wearing *me* out

M: Huh? (I should've been prepared for a retort, but...)

B: You're wearing me out, Dad. I'm wearing you in.

Not all of us relax in the same way.

Halftime Review
Age 3.5

Here were Benny's first several comments about Madonna's 2012 Super Bowl halftime show:

1) *She looks angry.*

2) *She's nice.*

3) *That looks like that Chipmunks movie.*

4) *That sounds like the first Fresh Beat Band song (a Nick, Jr. show).*

**Music (even Madonna, and The Chipmunks)
uniquely brings people together.**

Listening is Too Easy
Age 3.5

Benny's pre-school teacher gives stickers (most days) to the kids at the end of the day if they've listened well and followed directions. At one point, it seemed that Benny went a few weeks without getting any. Now, he's getting them more often than not. After getting one today, he turns to me and says, "Dad, listening is too easy."

Always encourage your kids (and yourself) to embrace new challenges.

Bad Cough
Age 3.5

For most of his early doctor's appointments, Benny barely uttered a few words to his doctor, who happens to be a good guy and reasonably friendly.

In Benny's defense, would *you* warm up to anyone who sticks you with a needle almost every time you meet?

On this particular appointment, Benny is more like the guy we see every day. When the doctor asks us how he's doing, Benny fake-coughs a time or two and answers, "I have a really bad cough, Dr. *Gullickson*."

As "they" say, humor is often the best medicine.

Okay, What is it, Daddy?
Age 3.5

I'm driving Benny to pre-school and we're playing 20 Questions, or whatever you call this game (Yes/No questions only). I'm thinking of a zebra. Here's the unofficial transcript:

Matt: Okay, Benny, it's an animal.

Benny: Is it a vehicle?

M: No.

B: Is it a person?

M: No.

B: Is it an animal?

M: Yes (however did he divine that?!)

B: (zeroing in) Does it live in the jungle?

M: YES!

(pretty good question for a not-yet-four-year-old newbie to this game)

B: Is it tall?

M: Y-yes.

B: Is it fast?

M: Yep—pretty fast. You're doing great.

B: Okay, what is it, Daddy?

If you have to surrender, do so on your own terms.

Sweet Appointment
Age 3.5

Ruby and I are trying to get Benny to cut down on junk food—
he has quite the sweet tooth. As with most kids, he likes it all.
Even lollipops from banks and doctors' offices.

Benny: Can I have some cookies?

Ruby: No, honey.

B: Oh, can I have some ice cream?

Matt: Sorry, you've been eating too many sweets.

B: I want some candy.

R: Honey...no!

B: Do I have a doctor's appointment today?

Use imagination and persistence to solve problems.

Being *Boyly-ish*
Age 3.5

We're in the drugstore, and Benny notices some birthday candleholders. He points to some Princess-themed ones, and says, "Hey Dad, these are girly-ish."

I reply, "Yeah, they are kind of girly."

Then he finds some 'Cars' ones and excitedly says, "Look, these are boyly-ish."

Amphibians
Age 3.5

I'm quizzing Benny about animals from the "Big Book of Animals" and he guesses frogs correctly. I come to the word *amphibian* and ask him, "An amphibian can live both here and here?"

Benny replies, "China and Cherry Hill, New Jersey."

That's my boy.

The answer is often better than the question.

So, keep asking questions.

Special Talent
Almost 4

Benny and I are discussing special talents; I'm not sure when this term first became a part of his working vocabulary.

Benny: My special talent is being a piano master, and Mommy's is cooking.

Matt: Great, Benny, but how about mine?

B: Your special talent is eating my Cheerios.

(Not *Special K?*)

M: Really? Is that my only special talent?

B: Dad, your other special talent is playing with me.

I'll take it.

Don't be afraid to share your special talents with the world.

Babies and Kids
Almost 4

Many have been the times that Ruby has called Benny "my baby", which admittedly doesn't always hit me the right way. I understand and appreciate that they have a type of connection that—as close as Benny and I am—we will never have. Still, it sometimes rubs me the wrong way when she says this.

Perhaps, it's my own insecurities at work.

Benny does a great job of reassuring me.

"Daddy, I'm Mommy's baby, and your kid."

We sometimes relate to the same people in slightly different ways.

Sweet Dreams
Almost 4

I'm still trying to make sense out of this Benny-ism.

Benny (just waking up, in a groggy voice): Dad, last night I dreamed about three things.

Matt: Really, what were they?

B (using his fingers): A helicopter, a race car and my Valentine's Day party.

M: Oh, how did you work all those things together?

B: Sometimes, I have bad dreams.

M: Okay, was this a bad dream?

B: I'm not supposed to have bad dreams.

M: Well—

B: I even dreamed about Spiderman.

M: Hey Benny, Wimbledon's coming on soon.

B: I also dreamed about an abacus, and even my McQueen puzzle.

Tangents are often more interesting than the main route.

Tricky Golf
Almost 4

We're casually watching golf and someone hits a marvelous approach shot that's tracking the hole for what would be an eagle. As it's bounding and rolling...

Matt: Benny, look at this! (It narrowly trickles past the hole.)

Benny: He missed.

M: Yeah, but you're not expected to make a shot from way out there. Look how close he came.

B: Golf is tricky, Dad.

M: It *is*. I was never a great golfer. I had a few good days, but—

B: ...but you never got it in the hole.

(I haven't played a round since a year or two before he was born. I conceded the point.)

It is often better to concede a point than to argue it. (That, and yours truly is not a very good golfer.)

The *Maleman*
Age 4

Benny, my just-turned four-year-old son, was captured giving a biology lecture to Ruby last night:

"Mom, you and 'Waipo' (Ruby's mom, his grandma) are females, and Daddy and I are males. But, I'm not really a male. The mailman doesn't pick me up."

One is never too old to learn, or too young to teach.

Avoiding Trouble
Age 4

I take him to the Discovery Museum and we bring just a little junk food for him. He eats it in the little snack area, right near the front door. When he's had enough, I ask him if he can stay there for about a minute while I run his water bottle and snack container to the car. A staff member says she'll keep an eye on him.

As I start to walk away, Benny— in a very loud voice— cautions, "Dad, try not to get into any trouble, okay?!" The ladies in the snack area and at the front desk crack up, as do I.

Benny keeps a straight face; maybe, he was being truthful.

Stay close to those you love (and also try to stay out of trouble).

Naked Truth
Age 4

Benny and his big cousin, Alex, usually get along well, but on this day, they're arguing a little, and doing a little name-calling. The names are mostly silly stuff, and not mean-spirited, and I observe a little before asking them to stop.

Alex: You're too little.

Benny: You're naked.

A: (surprised) You don't even know what naked means.

B: Yes, I do.

A: What?

B; It means that you don't have any clothes on.

A: (a little shocked, and dejected) Yeah, that's what it means.

When you issue a challenge to someone, don't be surprised when the challenge is met.

Squirrel Watch
Age 4

Benny: Mom, I saw a squirrel in the garden.

Ruby: Oh, really?

B: Yeah. It was eating one of your vegetables.

R: Oh, no.

B: It's okay, Mom. There's only one vegetable left.

When it comes to gardens and life, itself, always dwell on the bright side.

First Place
Age 4

Ruby and Benny had been away for a few days with her family, and Benny spent a lot of time with his (three-and-a-half years older) and much bigger cousin, Alex. Shortly after returning, he said:

B: Dad, I have good news and bad news.

M: What's the good news?

B; The good news is: Alex was a little bit nice to me.

M: Okay, what's the bad news?

B: He hit me a couple times.

M: Oh, do you know why he hit you?

B: I hit him first.

M: Benny, why did you hit him in the first place?

B: I hit him in the first place, and Alex hit me in the second place.

It's important to know your place(s).

Take My Website and Go Home
Age 4

I find a website that has cute animal pictures, and look at it with Benny. I ask him to tell a little story for each picture—if only a sentence or two— and he (predictably) is up for the task.

Each time, he begins with "Once upon a time..." and after five or six of these openings, I pretend to be annoyed, and react accordingly. One such reaction comes out a little harsh, and I laugh somewhat apologetically. Benny finds it funny as well.

We keep playing, and each time he starts with "Once upon a time," I interrupt him with my *annoyed* reaction. We continue the silly laughter. One of us is now enjoying this more than the other.

After five or so rounds of this, Benny puts an end to it. "Dad, if you keep ignoring me, I'm out of here."

What's amusing to you may not be amusing to others.

Hungry
Age 4

Benny has picked up a habit where he usually answers a question with "Well..."

It's somewhat endearing in normal conversations, and sometimes it even extends into the scenes (*movies*) that he will act out alone or with us. A typical role play scenario may unfold like this:

Benny: Dad, let's play Lion and T-Rex. Here, you be the lion.

Matt: Okay. (a brief silence)

B: Come on, Dad, you start.

M: *It's not easy being king of the jungle. Hey, what are you doing here?*

B: *Well—I'm just looking for something to eat.*

M: *You're pretty big. You're not thinking of eating me, are you?*

B: *Well—I'm thinking about it.*

M: (breaking character a bit): Wow, you are one introspective dinosaur. Do you know what introspective means?

B: *Well—I'm just hungry.*

It's not easy to distract a hungry carnivore,
yet it may be well worth the effort.

Tactical Error
Age 4

Benny is being his finicky self at the dinner table and Ruby and I are having little or no success convincing him to eat.

I decide to, if reluctantly, pull a trump card and mention that his big cousin Alex has always been a good eater. That's what I want to say, but here's the actual, terse conversation:

Matt: Benny, I don't really like to compare...

Benny: You *love* to compare.

(So much for that tactic)

Always be truthful, and consistent.

Calming Him Up
Age 4

It is one of those nights/early mornings when his energy knows no bounds. In fact, he is bounding and bouncing off the bed, and I can't get him to stop.

Matt: Benny, please calm down.

Benny: I don't want to calm down. I want to calm up.

It's okay to be left speechless, at times.

Supermarket Reading
Age 4

We make a quick shopping run to pick up a couple boxes of pasta and I'm pointing out how even when shopping, you have to use your reading skills. I'm reading the aisle signs and it goes something like this:

Matt: See, Benny, with almost everything you do in life—not only in school—you have to use your reading skills: whether shopping, driving or reading books. You can read everything...

Benny: Yeah, Dad, and I can read the books with all the bad words.

As I am rendered almost speechless beyond a bewildered "What bad words?", a man overhears our little exchange and as he wheels by, turns to me and says, "Hey, good luck with that one."

Give your children the tools to succeed, and hope that they use them as you intended.

Ancient History
Age 4

Benny: Dad, do you know what ancient means?

Matt: I used to (going for irony).

B: No, really.

M: It means old.

B: No.

M: It means really, really, really old?

B: Yes.

M: So, Benny can you name something that is ancient?

B: How about my old basketball game?

M: No, you've kind of outgrown it, but it's not ancient.

B: My old toys.

M: Nah, not really. I don't know if there's anything really ancient around here.

B: How about your underwear?

Age is a relative matter.

Going Crazy
Age 4

Benny and Ruby are in the car driving to the supermarket, and he keeps asking her, "Where are we going? Where are we going, Mommy?" Ruby is thinking about something else, and doesn't say anything, so Benny gives himself a good answer "I think we're going crazy, Mommy. I think we're going crazy!"

Don't be in a hurry to reach every destination.

Awesome Man
Age 4

One summer evening, we go out (around 9:30 pm) for a gelati; he is in one of his talkative moods. After *reassuring* the couple next to us that he'll still be up for another couple hours, the following quick dialogue ensues:

Matt: So Ben, are we gonna read a book together tonight?

Benny: Yes, we are.

M: What are we gonna read?

B: 'Awesome Man.'

M: Sounds good.

B: Oh, Dad? Dad?!

M: Yes.

B: Is Awesome Man overdue yet?

(No, but we're working on it.)

It's awesome to share with others, and to return what you've borrowed in a timely manner.

They tell us that we, as parents, are supposed to have all the answers. Who are they, and what do they know that we don't?

Laurel Acres Liaison
Age 4

One afternoon, I take Benny to a local park (Laurel Acres), where he meets a six-year-old girl named *Julia*. The two really take to each other and play together the rest of the day.

About a week later, Ruby takes Benny to the same park and mentions that he played with a slightly older girl named Julia who after playing with him for awhile came up to her and *confessed*, "I really like your son."

Play with others in a way that they will want to play with you again.

Swing Man
Age 4

We drive to the playground on the way back from some errands.

Benny spots a young girl out of the car window as we pull up. His exact quote, "Hey Dad, there's a little girl on the swings. I better go introduce myself."

Don't wait for others to introduce themselves first.

Remote Poppings
Age 4

Recently, I had asked Benny how he knew so much about everything, and he said, "Things just pop into my head." He likes to turn the tables on us and vice versa.

Benny: Dad, why did you say "Explore your dinner?"

Matt: I don't know. It just popped into my head,

B: Things don't pop into a grownup's head.

M: Why not?

B: Because grownups are the bosses.

M: So, things can't pop into a boss's head?

B: No.

M: Why?

B: Because they are in charge of the town.

M: So, if I were in charge of the town, wouldn't I want things to pop into my head?

B: (starts to demonstrate with toy cars on the dining room table before losing some interest) Let's say there were two cars and the one was the boss, and—Dad, the sofa is also very crowded, there's lots of remotes and books and toys, and...

There's an art to skillfully deflecting tough questions.

Pre-Garden
Age 4

Ruby: How was your first day of pre-school?

Benny: But I'm in kindergarten

R: No, you'll be there next year. You're still in Pre-K.

B (a little sad): You mean, I'm not a garden? I'm a pre-garden?

Student/Child/Kid
Age 4

Matt: Benny, what's the difference between a student, a child and a kid?

Benny: A student is someone who has a teacher who teached him.

M: Good, and a child?

B: A child is someone who is little and grows and grows and grows.

M: And...

B: A kid plays and eats and plays some more and sleeps.

Nurture your inner child: Don't neglect the importance of playing, eating and sleeping enough!

Just Two Little Things
Age 4

I hate to brag, but this whole parenting thing is getting ridiculously easy. What's so tricky about it?

In fact, after just a little bit of reflection, prayer and communication, Ruby and I have found that we always have all the right answers. Okay, more accurately, there are only two potential situations out of the whole week when Benny gives us any difficulties whatsoever.

1. When he's awake

2. When he's asleep

See You in Excember
Age 4

Matt: So, Benny, did you know when Plish (our pet betta fish)'s birthday is? Isn't it around today? (to Ruby) Honey, didn't we get him around September last year?

Ruby: Yes, I think so.

Benny: No, no. It was in Excember.

M: Excember? When's that?

B: It's in the Spring.

Don't be bound by everyone else's expectations of time.

Toastmasters Meeting
Age 4

(This may appeal mostly to fellow Toastmasters, if hopefully, not exclusively so.)

The other day, Benny and I were taking a walk around a small lake, er glorified creek, and lots of ducks and geese were congregating nearby. I mentioned something very *scientific* to Benny, such as, "See, look, they're talking to each other."

Benny: Hey, Dad, they're having a Toastmasters meeting.

Sharing and Sparing
Age 4

After his pre-school class, Benny shared a story about sharing.

Benny: *Andrew* shared his "Toy-Mater" (Tow-Mater?) with *Robert*, and *Robert* was playing with it and didn't want to give it back.

Matt: Oh, why not?

B: Because he wanted to take it home. But then he just took it—

M: Who?

B: *Andrew*.

M: Oh, okay. And then what happened?

B: Well, I started playing with it.

M: How did you end up with it?

B: I just saw it there, and then *Andrew* put it in his backpack, but a marble fell out and this girl was playing with it.

M: And—

B: Well, he put it back in his backpack.

M: Put what?

B: The marble.

M: But, how about Toy-Mater?

B: Dad, that was already in his backpack.

M: Oh, then what happened?

B: That's the end of my story, Dad.

A Whale of a Conversation
Age 4

On the way home from pre-school and a little playground time, we enjoyed a long conversation.

Matt: Benny, are you hungry?

Benny: I'm so hungry I can eat a whale the size of a tomato. (The light bulb goes off.) Hey, "whale" and "tomato" rhyme; I hear the same sound.

M: They kind of do. But where can we find a whale the size of a tomato?

B: In the sea.

M: Okay. Hey, didn't you just learn about 'Jonah and the Whale' yesterday?

(Benny had his first day (ever) of Hebrew School the day before.)

B: Yeah.

M: So, what happened in the story? (Truthfully, I didn't remember.)

B: The whale ate Jonah. And now, he's a happy whale.

M: But, how about Jonah? Was he happy?

B: Yes, he listened to God's word.

M: What did God say to him?

B: I don't know.

Engage your kids in conversation. You may even be rewarded with a whale of a story.

Air Mattress
Age 4

I drop Ruby and Benny off (along with Ruby's mom) to JFK Airport for their long (about 16-hours, non-stop) flight to China. I'm not able to attend the long stay there, and will miss them terribly. Here is a short part of my conversation with Benny.

Matt: So Benny, you'll enjoy the airplane. You can watch movies, or just take a nap—

Benny: They have beds on the plane?

Communicate clearly, so you don't set false expectations.

15 Minutes of...?
Age 4

While Benny and Ruby are away in China, I try to catch them over the phone around 11 am Eastern Time. It's exactly 11 hours later in China, and this kid never goes to bed (on any continent or planet that I'm aware of) before 11 pm.

Matt: Benny, did you take a shower tonight?

Benny: No Dad, I'm still dirty.

M: How much longer are you going to be dirty?

B: Well...................15 more minutes.

Don't let your plans get washed away too soon.

Bad Connection
Age 4

Ruby and Benny flew into Ruby's hometown from another city in China last night, but are now without a cell phone to be able to call outside of China. Her sister informs me that they have arrived safely at this destination, and I try to reach them at their hotel. It takes me awhile to communicate their extension to the hotel receptionist, (yes, my "grasp" of Mandarin is as poor as ever) so I am relieved, and a little surprised, to soon hear Ruby's voice.

She hands the phone to Benny. He comes on, and the first thing he says is, "Dad, I can't hear you. I think we have a bad connection again." He walks away, and Ruby picks up.

I get Benny back and tell him that I picked up some new Halloween books to read to him over the phone. Alas, there's no time to read to him now, as Ruby's aunt and uncle arrive to take them out to eat.

There have been more tricks than treats this Halloween, but at least they're safe and Benny's as cool and unpredictable as ever.

Black and Black
Age 4

We're doing some kind of verbal roleplay. I think Benny's himself and I'm the neighbor's dog's owner. It started when we were acting out a likely scenario from a book called "Can I Pet Your Dog?"

Benny: We got a new oven and dishwasher.

Matt: Oh, what colors are they?

B: Black and black.

M: Good. What happened to the old ones?

B: Actually, they weren't working.

M: What was wrong with them?

B: The doors wouldn't open, so me and Mommy buyed these.

Dinner for Two?
Age 4

It's sometimes—okay, almost always—quite a chore for us to get Benny to sit and eat a good meal. Tonight, he got out of his chair in mid-plate and announced, "Hey guys, I hope you enjoy your dinner without your son."

Meals are more enjoyable when shared with those we love. At the same time, it is just sustenance, right?

Benny's Playmate
Age 4

Benny really likes this pre-school classmate of his (named *Audrey*). I ask him about his school day.

Matt: Did you go to the playground today?

Benny: Yes.

M: So, who did you play with?

B: Audrey.

M: Does she like the playground, too?

B: Yes.

M: What does she enjoy playing?

B: (with a slightly impish smile): She likes to play with me.

College Memories
Age 4

We're watching some animated movie with mice on TV—I forget which one.

Matt: Hey Ben, did I ever tell you this story?

Benny: What story, Dad?

M: When I was in college, my last year, six of us lived in a house together.

B: (with exaggerated enthusiasm) Really? What happened next? Tell me!

M: So, there were six of us and—

B: What were their names?!

M: Okay, there was Dave, Jeff, David, but he had a nickname, a guy we called Sloth and another nicknamed Rat. And Rat had a cat in the house.

B: What did he do?

M: Well, one day, I put on my bathrobe and the cat had put a dead mouse in the pocket. So, guess what I did?

B: You flushed it down the toilet?

M: The robe?

B: No, the dead mouse, silly.

M: I don't think so.

B: You threw it in the trash can and then flushed it down the toilet.

M: Of course.

The best told stories of mice and men
sometimes change over the years.

Little Sir Echo
Age 4

Is it just me, or does anybody else hear an echo?

Matt: Benny, what is the main difference between China and the United States?

Benny: Benny, what is the main difference between China and the United States?

M: No, really, what's—

B: No, really, what's—

M: So... how's your pizza?

B: So...how's your pizza?

M: Okay, you win.

B: Okay, I win.

If you want someone to agree with you, tell them what you think they want to hear.

Gift Consultant
Age 4

We're looking for a birthday card, and later a present, for a classmate who has a fifth birthday party the next day.

Looking at cards:

Benny: Dad, let's get her this dinosaur card.

Matt: I don't know. Do you think she'll like it? Is she a girly girl?

B: Nah, she's a boyly girl.

Now looking at books:

I give him a choice of two books to 'join' another we agreed on—one of them has a spinner, which he chooses.

M: Is that the one you think she'll prefer?

B: Yeah. I think she'll like that one with the spinner.

M: Why?

M: All five-year-old girls like to do ballet.

So if you're shopping for a birthday present for a young girl, be sure to remember this advice.

Spilt Cookie
Age 4

I'm not sure if this is a Benny-ism or a *Family-Clumsy-ism.*

Benny and I have a one-to-two-year tradition of going to Barnes & Noble and splitting a Starbucks Triple Chocolate Chunk (TCC) cookie. I usually get a few B&N gift cards per year as presents from my students/families and they're used almost exclusively for this purpose.

One afternoon, we visit the Cherry Hill store but there are no TCCs in the case. Dilemma! We debate whether to get the peanut butter or sugar cookies, as the next batch of TCC cookies were just made, and would need 45 or so minutes to cool. We get a hot chocolate to split and decide to wait on our favorite treat. After one little sip apiece, Benny then spills the hot chocolate (luckily, it wasn't *too* hot) all over himself. We go home without our favorite treat.

Note: It comes to mind that he likes hot ice cream and cold chocolate.

One week later, we go to the Mt. Laurel store. Benny inspects the dessert case—only one TCC is left, but there are five people ahead of us in line. He 'guards' the case and asks me to do the same. When we arrive at the front of the line, the TCC is still there, he orders it, and asks me for the gift card. Now as luck, fate and my clumsiness would have it, on my hurried trip to the table, the TCC slides off the plate like a greased pig on Teflon.

Benny: (in a voice that could be heard in Philly): Dad, it fell on the floor—are we still gonna eat it?

(I shouldn't reveal my incriminating answer, but yes, that cookie...still....tasted quite good. And amazingly, neither of us spilled our water.)

A sweet tooth and an impatient nature can lead to unhealthy results.

Airplane Hypothetical
Age 4

Thankfully. Benny is not even close to being a bully, but he's human—and will sometimes grab or push or hit his friends. So, I was just talking to him about it and how he should never hit or push—especially anyone smaller or younger than him.

Benny: So, what if there's a rough kid?

Matt: What do you mean?

B: What if there's a rough kid who hits me?

M: Are you talking in general or about a specific example?

B: What does 'specific' mean?

M: Oh—something that actually happened.

B: Like the Specific Ocean?

M: No, I was thinking about the *Spatlantic*.

A few moments later, he has a "Pacific" example.

B: What if I'm flying on an airplane and some kid hits me in the nose?

Superpowers
Age 4

(A mini-Benny-ism just now, from the toilet.) Benny knows I'm flying to Israel the next day, and will be gone for a little while.

Benny: Dad, I wish you can fly through the phone so you can be here with me.

Matt: That's very nice, Benny, but how can I do that?

B: (motioning with his hands in a serpentine pattern): Just get a map and use your superpowers.

If only.

We all need to feel like a superhero at times. How do we achieve that status? It all starts with love and kindness.

Health Nut
Age 4

Benny is choosing his snack for pre-school today (his class runs from 1-3:30 pm). He passes up a big box of cookies.

Benny: (proudly) I'm not gonna have any of these cookies, or cheese crackers. They're junk food. I'm bringing these (picks up a pack of salty pretzels).

When you make a good choice, be proud of it.

Tour Guide
Age 4.5

I'm telling Ruby and Benny about a tour of a guide dog training facility that I took in Israel. The tour guide (not the canine one) was very good, and her English was terrific, but not flawless. She wanted us to take a look in the bathroom, but instead said, "Please poke your head in the toilet for a minute."

Benny: So, did you do it?

Matt: No, I didn't. Should I have?

B: Yes, you should always follow your teacher.

M: Even then?

B: Not if it's a bad teacher because your whole body would have been flushed away (makes sound effects).

Good to be back home.

Fake Tough
Age 4.5

We're watching (the original) *Lady and the Tramp,* which in my opinion, is Disney's best animated film. The scene comes where Lady is being cornered by three big, menacing (hyena-like) stray dogs. Tramp suddenly appears and starts fighting them off. During this scene, I ask my four-and-a-half year-old:

Matt: Wow, is Tramp really that tough?

Benny: No, but he's trying to be.

Self-belief is the first step toward achieving something great.

Line Leadership
Age 4.5

On the way home from pre-school, I asked Benny about his day. It took him a little while to give any details, preferring to say "I don't know", blended together like one word, "Idono." And then, he finally remembered and in an excited tone, said:

Benny: Oh Dad, I was the line leader today.

Matt: Oh, really? That's great.

B: Yeah, I thought they would never, ever pick me.

M: How did they pick you?

B: They just drew my stick. I saw the B-e-n-n-y word and knew it was me.

M: So what did you do?

B: I lined up on Number One.

M: So, you did number one? (Nobody said I wasn't childlike, or a little immature.)

B: No.

M: You did number two?

B: No. I just led them out the door.

M: So where did you take them?

B: To the bathroom, silly....

Finding Nemo
Age 4.5

I'm glad my son is honest—(good parenting?) —but sometimes I wish he could keep silly secrets just a little longer. Benny had already established that my "special talent" was eating his foods—such as cereal, cookies and peanut butter.

So he announces, "Dad, you keep eating my peanut butter. I'm gonna hide it...in my Nemo lunch bag on the kitchen table."

If you err, err on the side of too much honesty (and overfeeding those you love).

Like a Pro
Age 4.5

Today, Benny earned his "Zip up like a Pro" distinction on the classroom bulletin board for being able to—for the first time—put on and zip his jacket by himself. At dinner, I was giving him names of real people and fake characters alike, and asking him what they do like a pro.

Matt: Ms. *Peters* (his pre-school teacher)

Benny: She teaches us things like a pro.

M: Wile E. Coyote

B: Killing the Roadrunner, trying to destroy it and trying to find it.

M: How about the Roadrunner?

B: Making the Coyote lose.

M: Mommy

B: Gives me lots of love

M (tempting fate): How about me?

B: (in an almost stern voice): You use your laptop too much—like a pro

As I start to laugh, Benny adds: "Okay, let's not talk about pros anymore; let's talk about dinosaurs, okay?"

Role Reversal
Age 4.5

Benny: Hey Dad, did you put that tissue on the floor?

Matt: Well, I didn't put it there, but it must have fallen out of my pocket.

B: Please throw it out.

M: (I did.) Hey, did you just become my Dad? (No immediate reply, so I explore further) What would it be like it you were my dad and I was your son?

B (warming to the scenario): Then, Mommy and I would be your boss.

M: What if I didn't listen, or follow directions?

B: I'd have to give you a time out.

M: What if I followed directions really well?

B: Then, I'd give you a time in.

We learn compassion when we wear other people's shoes.

World's Best Swimmers
Age 4.5

Benny and I are driving home from karate class, and he mentions that he wants to start taking swimming lessons. He took a class or two when he was one, and as a "big boy" he reasoned that he should really learn how. I agree, and then he steers our conversation like this:

Benny: Dad, mermaids are the best swimmers.

Matt: Why are they so good?

B: Because they have tails and live in the water.

M: Okay, who are the second best swimmers?

B: A scuba diver. Dad, what's a scuba diver?

M: They dive underwater to explore, with special gear on. Who's next?

B: Submarines.

M: They're not people. But, okay.

B: Dad, how about my bath toys?

M: Sure, why not. They're number four. Can we add one more and make it a top five?

B: Fishes.

M: Great list. Can you tell us the top five again?

B: Sure, number one is mermaids. Then scuba divers. Submarines. And then my bath toys and then fishes.

Who could argue with that list?

President Daddy
Age 4.5

I believe this one started with a President's Day commercial on TV—probably for a car dealership.

Matt: Benny, who's your favorite President?

Benny: Take a guess.

M: Is it George Washington?

B: No.

M: Abraham Lincoln?

B: No.

M: President Obama?

B: No.

M: Okay, who is it?

B: *You* are, when you speak as President of your Toastmasters club.

Use your power of free speech to speak well of others.

No Obstruction
Age 4.5

Benny and I are driving home from New York City. He notices some cool stuff from his rear window.

Benny: Hey Dad, look at that instruction.

Matt: You mean **con**struction.

B: What does instruction mean?

M: **In**struction is like directions that you have to follow. **Con**struction is what *Bob the Builder* does.

B: Are there any other –struction words?

M: There's **de**struction...like what *Wreck-it Ralph* did when he destroyed buildings. (Benny and I saw the movie. Well, he fell asleep, and I, unfortunately, stayed with it.)

B: No, that's **un**struction.

Of Mice and Men
Age 4.5

This morning, an uninvited mouse invaded our kitchen. Benny and Ruby are discussing this situation.

Benny: Mom, do you need to pick up some toys for me—and what else?

Ruby: I have to pick up some mousetraps.

B: But we have those sticky mousetraps.

R: Yeah, but I want to get more. We need more.

B: But mice like Swiss cheese; they don't like mozzarella cheese.

R: Okay. I will give them cheese and some bread.

B: They also like some bread? How did you know that? Did you just look it up online?

Make every effort to serve your guests (even the uninvited ones) what they like to eat.

The Scientist
Age 4.5

Benny: Dad, when I grow up, I want to be a scientist.

Matt: That's great. What type of scientist do you want to be?

B: A regular one. The main one.

M: What does the main scientist do?

B: They learn about science.

M: What type of science?

B: I don't know. Hey, I can study about dinosaurs.

M: Good idea. What do they call the scientists that study the dinosaurs?

B: Paleon—

M: Like aliens?

B: Paleontologists.

M: That's right. So maybe you can discover why the dinosaurs became extinct?

B: Why did they?

M: I don't know. That's your job.

B: Maybe they ruled the earth long enough and now other animals ruled the earth.

M: Like which animals?

B: The lizards, the turtles, lions, zebras, horses and doggies. Everything. Warthogs.

M: So, the dinosaurs just gave up their kingdom? Willingly?

B: Yes, they were taking turns.

The importance of taking turns, socially and historically, cannot be overstated.

Food Groups
Age 4.5

We're discussing eating healthier ... something I definitely don't always exemplify. I tell him that neither of us should be eating from the following "basic food groups" every day: cereal, pizza, Cocoa Puffs and candy.

Benny's irrefutable logic?

"So, if we shouldn't eat candy every day, we should eat it every night?"

A determined mind will always find a way to his destination.

Split Hairs, not Teeth
Age 4.5

Ruby and I are both with Benny in the waiting room of his dentist. It's been about a 12-minute wait—not too bad. He doesn't mind. He's not looking forward to getting a cavity filled, and there's stuff to do in the waiting room.

Suddenly we hear: "For Benny Goldberg."

Me: Okay, Benny, let's go. They're ready for you.

Benny: No, Dad. They said, *For Benny*, not *Benny*.

Logically, semantically, he was right, but it didn't excuse him from his appointment.

Believing the Skype
Age 4.5

I'm telling Benny about a radio show I did the night before. I was the guest on a show that was broadcast via a website—with the ability for it to be archived and played at any future point.

Matt: It was a little different because I couldn't see who I was talking to.

Benny: You just talked over the phone?

M: Yep, just like talking to a friend or one of my brothers. But, I couldn't see anyone, so it was different from other types of speaking I do.

B: But you do Toastmasters.

M: I do. And there, there are people to talk to, or *perform* for. Here, I had to try to time when to start and when to stop without seeing anyone.

B: Why don't they just use Skype? Don't they know how to?

Learning isn't always conveyed from teacher to student or from parent to child. Learning happens in all directions, both formally and informally, by design and accident alike.

The Cat and the Fruit
Age 4.5

A quick conversation with Benny—with the TV on in the background:

Matt: Oh man, I just forgot to save a file I was working on last night and now I have to re-do it.

Benny: Was it "A Snowball's Chance" (my previous co-authored book) related?

M: Yeah, mostly.

B: That's becoming my favorite book a little bit.

M: Thanks, Benn—

B (not one to dwell on the topic at hand, unless he's dwelling on the topic at hand): Dad, look, The Cat in the Hat is wearing three silly fruits on his head.

Sometimes, as parents, we'll be (seemingly) relegated to second banana status behind TV, movie and book characters. Don't worry; it's only temporary.

The Wordapod Master
Age 4.5

I opened the door to check on Benny and he immediately says:

Benny: I just invented a new word called "watermorphosis."

(And then, before I could ask him about it)

B: It means to sink in the water.

Yes, I am the "inventor" of 300 or so Wordapods (neologisms, if you prefer), but I bow to the young prodigy.

Show your kids the way, and if they outdo you, so much the better.

Book Covers
Age 4.5

Benny had mentioned—about a week ago—that an author/illustrator had visited their pre-school, and I 'Googled' her image and asked him to guess who it was.

Benny: That's Barbara McClintock

Matt: Wow, how did you know?

B: Dad, she's an illustrator. She writes the words.

M: Well, actually, as an illustrator, she does the art work. But sometimes—

B: I know.

M: Benny, is this the woman who came to your school?

B: No, she was in the gym.

M: The gym's at your school, right?

B: Dad, I want to see some of her book covers.

Singing *Stevie*
Age 4.5

Benny and I are discussing his day in pre-school.

Benny: Dad, everyone was there today except for *Stevie*.

Matt: Oh, where was Stevie?

B: I don't know. But that's kind of a good thing.

M: Why would you say—

B: He always ruins my songs.

M: What do you mean?

B: When I'm singing a song, he never sings the right words.

M: Can you give me an example?

B: I don't know.

M: What is a song that you sing?

B: I start singing, "It's raining, it's pouring. Monster Max is boring."

M: What does Stevie sing?

B: He just ruins it.

M: What does he do?

B: He just starts singing silly words.

M: Well, does he have a good voice, at least?

B: Kind of good.

M: That's good.

B: No, not really...I said "kind of good."

M: Okay, so who's the best singer in the class?

B: Everyone but Stevie.

Not everyone can be the best at everything, right?

Hide and Seek a Book
Age 4.5

I'm at the library with Benny and he's sitting at one of the tables doing a magnetic puzzle when a girl of about the same age (it turns out she's two months older) approaches him. "Will you play with me?" A smile lights up his face and I suggest that he introduce himself to her.

"What's your name?" Benny asks.

"I'm Zoe."

I encourage Benny to tell her his name.

"I'm Benny."

They start to play some game that she comes up with (she brought a little horse) when she suggests that they now play hide-and-seek.

Benny replies, "Hide-and-seek is an outdoor game. We're indoors."

As the only parent on the scene (the girl's mom or dad never materialized while we were there) I assure him that they can play as long as they stay away from the stairs or elevator and don't run too fast or yell too loud. It is the children's floor of the library.

The game's going well, although Benny proves to be a slightly better seeker than hider. The popular areas to hide are behind or under the kiddie book holders that are in the shape of animals.

Zoe—who was only counting to 10—now counts up to 25 (skipping 19 and 20) and Benny finds his favorite spot. After about five seconds of not being found, he becomes impatient.

"I'm here. Find me. I'm under the rhino's butt."

Hiding seldom solves your problems, especially if your hiding place is under a rhino's butt.
Think about it...if you wish.

Field of Dads
Age 4.5

Matt: Hey, would you like to watch a little of "Field of Dreams?"

Benny: Can we watch "A Christmas Story" on Chanukah?

M: Yeah, why not. There really aren't any Chanukah movies. I always wanted to write one.

B: How about "Life of God?"

M: Hmmm—why Life of God?

B: Because God's Jewish.

M: Hmmm (my favorite response for these head scratchers)

B: But God didn't really make the people.

M: He didn't?

B: No, he made the towns and buildings and then the people moved into the houses.

M: So, should we watch a little Field of Dreams?

B: How about Field of Dads?

When conversing with someone that has a fertile mind, it's okay to give him the last word.

Collection of Dads
Age 4.5

With Ruby away and my being under the weather (bad sinusitis, which I'm prone to), I apologized for being a little boring the last couple days.

Benny: Yeah, you've been Boring Dad.

Matt: I have been Boring Dad.

B: You've been Boring Dad, Tough Dad and Fat Dad.

M: All those—at the same time?!

B: Yeah, I have a whole collection of Dads.

Losing His Patience
Age 4.5

I'm not sure if the following short anecdote is more a commentary on: a) my inability to learn Chinese; b) Benny not having enough patience to one day be a teacher or c) both.

This morning, Ruby said something in Chinese to Benny that he laughed at. Feeling left out, I asked Benny what "Mommy" said.

Benny replies to me, "I don't want to teach you that Chinese expression because you're just going to ruin it."

(That's never my intention, although the boy makes a good point.)

Patience is a virtue, but impatience usually begets more impatience.

Thingamajigger
Age 4.5

We sometimes play a game called "thingamajigger" in which we start with an object and have to come up with various creative uses for it. This morning, I picked up a cheap piece of metal—it's maybe one inch in diameter—not sure where it came from.

Matt: Thingamajigger (putting it over my finger): My new wedding ring.

Benny: Thingamajigger: A boomerang (hope there's no correlation)

M: Thingamajigger: It's a halo.

B: Thingamajigger: It's a hula hoop for—a mouse.

M: Thingamajigger: It's a Frisbee.

B: Thingamajigger (raising it between his eyes): Glasses for a Cyclops.

Game, Set, Match to Benny.

The irrelevance of mythology is simply a myth.

Knock-Knock
Age 4.5

Benny's telling me about something that happened in school the day before.

Benny: Dad, we were playing knock-knock jokes, but *Jimmy* kept cheating.

Matt: How do you cheat at knock-knock?

B: Whenever someone said "knock-knock", Jimmy would just keep saying, "Who's there?"

M: Can you give me an example?

B: Well, I'd say "knock-knock", and he'd say, "Who's there?" "Who's there?" "Who's there?" Who's..."

M: Okay, that might be annoying, but how's it cheating? It's not a game that someone can win, is it?

B: Yes.

M: Well, how do you decide who wins?

B: Whoever comes up with the best knock-knock joke wins.

M: So, who won?

B: (smiles, and shrugs his shoulder) I dunno.

M: Did *you* win?

B: No, we didn't have time to finish the game.

M: How many kids were playing?

B: Everyone at the blue table.

M: So, do you want to play now?

B: Okay. Knock-knock.

M: Who's there? Who's there? Who's there? Who's...

B: You're cheating, Dad.

In games, as in life in general, there are official rules and self-made rules of convenience. Both have their place.

Very Fetching
Age 4.5

Benny brings a toy to the school playground (a Bakugan ball) and his friend, *Kenny*, wants to play with it. He's trying to grab it from Benny, and his mom objects and tells him he's wrong. I more-or-less take up for Kenny, reminding Benny that he's played with his friend's toys before and that he should share. I ask Benny to ask his friend's mom if he can ask Kenny if he'd like to play with the ball. (Sorry for that long sentence.)

Benny does. Kenny does. It's all good until Benny wants to play with it again. He asks Kenny if he could have it back, and his friend obliges. Sort of. He tells Benny that he has to chase it. He then throws it several feet away, and says, "Fetch it."

My son—insisting on receiving his proper dignity—replies, "Don't treat me like a dog."

Alas, Benny does go fetch, er, pick it up and continues to play until—the next little dispute.

Always respect the dignity of those around you, regardless of age or any other factor.

A New Dessert
Age 4.5

Benny just now—eagerly awaiting his dessert.

"Mommy, is this popcorn on the cob?"

A Fake Dessert
Age 4.5

We're at the park, and a few girls who are selling cake pops approach us. I can't resist, even though I had never seen these cakes-on-a-stick before. I give one to Benny, who keeps saying, while giggling, "For real, it's fake." The girls get a kick out of that.

After they leave, I ask Benny, "If you said *For fake, it's real*, is it fake or real?"

Benny: It's fake.

Matt: Right. How about *For fake, it's fake*?

B: It's fake.

M: No, that would make it real. I was starting to explain about double negatives and all that, and then remembered he wasn't yet 5.

After a pause, Benny says, "If you say, "For real, it's real, then it's real."

United Nations
Age 4.5

Benny and Ruby are shopping in a department store looking for a baseball cap to give to one of his friends for his birthday. They ask one of the employees for assistance, but his words are a little hard for them to decipher. He appears to be speaking in a heavy Indian accent.

Said our very culturally sensitive almost-five-year-old linguist, "Mommy, he's speaking Spanish. We don't understand Spanish."

It's always good to know what you don't know. Now, use that knowledge as a springboard to learn more.

Well-Placed Emotion
Age 4.5

A momentous day in the young life of Benny—he had his last day of pre-school and his last game as a member of the Muckdogs (first year of tee-ball).

Here's an unofficial transcript of the family exit interview /debriefing session:

Matt: Benny, how do you feel about playing your last game as a Muckdog?

Benny: Happy.

M: Really? Why?

B: Because I don't like to exercise and sweat.

M: How do you feel about no more pre-school?

B: Sad.

Ruby: Did you cry?

B: What are you talking about?!

It's okay to cry sometimes. Really. By the same token, don't accuse someone of crying when they haven't.

Goodness of His Heart
Almost 5

Ruby takes Benny to a casual play date with a friend. He brings along a toy (the sheriff-mobile from *Cars*) to give to his friend, somewhat surprising and impressing the other boy's mom. She thanks him, and then Benny blows his cover just a little.

Says the generous Benny: Yeah, I don't like that toy anymore.

As a rule, honesty is always best, but too much honesty can devalue your own act of generosity.

Syrup
Almost 5

This morning, at breakfast, I pour the maple syrup over my pancakes in a smiley face pattern and point it out to Benny.

Benny: It doesn't have a nose.

Matt: It doesn't need a nose; it's a smiley face.

B: But how will it smell?

M: It doesn't need to smell; it just needs to smile. It's a smiley face—not a smelly face.

(I found myself actually winning one of these father-son debates.)

B: But Dad, it needs a nose.

M: Why?

B: Because.

M: "Because" isn't an answer—it just tells us that there's a good reason coming.

(pause)

M: Look, let's bring up Google Images. You'll see that the classic smiley face doesn't have a nose.

B: Okay.

I bring the laptop over. Out of a whole page of smiley faces without eyes, *his* eyes go right to the one Sponge Bob smiley face that shows a little nose.

B: See, Dad. Sponge Bob's smiley face has a nose. So, next time you make one out of maple syrup, don't forget the nose, okay?

(The silence of resignation.)

Just one little piece of evidence can invalidate an otherwise strong argument.

Challenging
Almost 5

Benny worked on some writing and early math exercises this summer. The current book is supposedly for Grade 1 and called the "Place Value Zoo." He did pretty well with it this day.

Benny: Dad, these were all easy pages. Why?

Matt: Because you're smart. But, I can always add some stuff to make it more challenging.

B: Good. I love to be challenged. (He sounds sincere, and it's almost scary.)

M: Okay, I challenge you to clean up all your toys and your bedroom.

B: (laughing): That's not a challenge.

M: Sure it is. Why not?

B: It's just not a challenge.

M: It is—what do you mean?

B: No, it's only a challenge when it's a game.

Supercroc
Age 5

I've never been that great at science, but luckily, there's Benny around to fill in some gaps.

Benny: Dad, do you know Supercroc?

Matt: The shoe, or the crocodile?

B: Supercroc was from the Triassic Time Period.

M: Oh, the shoe. No, never heard of him.

B: He was able to eat a whole Argentinosaurus. Lots of.

M: Really?

B: Yes.

M: Is that why the dinosaurs became extinct?

B: Yeah.

M: So, what would Supercroc have for a typical breakfast?

B: Dinosaurs.

M: How many?

B: One hundred—I mean ten hundred.

There you have it, fellow paleontologists.

Steely Ben
Age 5

I play a Steely Dan song (called *Black Cow*) on YouTube, and ask him if he likes it.

Benny: Is that the Beatles?

(We only listen to "current" stuff 'round here.)

Matt: No, it's a group called Steely Dan. They combined jazz and rock-and-roll.

B: I don't like jazz.

M: Why not?

B: 'cause I like rock-and-roll and disco.

(Oy, I don't want to disown him over disco, but...)

M: Why do you like disco?

B: Because I like how it sounds.

M: How does it sound?

B: (Almost striking a pose) Chu-chu-chu-chu chu-chu-chu (something like that)

M: How does rock-and-roll sound?

B: (air guitar mode) nare-nare-nare-nare-nare...

M: Okay, how about jazz?

B: It's a little hard to describe.

Some wonderful things just have to be experienced.

Reality TV
Age 5

We're half-watching "The Cat in the Hat" (TV show) when Benny...

Benny: This is fictional because the porcupine is talking.

Matt (stunned by the news): What's fictional?

B: "The Cat in the Hat."

M: Oh, just because of the porcupine?

B: No, cats can't talk, but the Cat-in-the-Hat can.

M: How about Nick and Sally?

B: The people are real.

Reality, like beauty, is sometimes in the eye(s) of the beholder.

4-H Club
Age 5

In the car, on the way to the shore, I ask Ruby and Benny if they'd like to hear anything about a new-ish presentation I've been working on. Essentially, it involves what I call "The Four Hs of Dynamic Presentations".

Benny (who has helped me by listening and reacting to other speeches for competitions): Yeah, what is it, Dad?

Matt: Okay, I talk about the 4 Hs, which are: Humility, Heart, Honesty and Humor.

B: Wait, Dad. "Honesty" doesn't start with an "H"—the others are okay.

(Not quite true, but also not bad for a just-turned-five-year-old boy)

Educated Fish
Age 5

Benny and his cousin Alex are about to go to the aquarium with Ruby, and he's talking about schools of fish.

Matt: So, you mean that fish go to school? Do some of them go to school—even kindergarten like you?

Benny: No, not that type of school. It's like when a bunch of animals all group together to be safe.

M: Like Nemo?

B: Kind of. They all try to stay safe.

M: From who?

B: From their predators.

M: Benny, I hope that you'll always be fascinated by science and the animal world.

B: I don't really know that much about science. I like it a little bit, but don't really know how to do it. I just like watching it.

The best way to learn (and to teach) is to involve all the senses.

The Joy of Nothingness
Age 5

I ask Benny if his "K" class has line leaders, like they did last year in pre-school. Today is his fourth afternoon of "K."

Benny: Kind of.

Matt: What do you mean?

B: They don't call them that.

M: What do they call them?

B: Nothing.

M: Have you been a "nothing" this year?

B: No, I never get to be a nothing.

M: So, what do you do?

B: I just line up with all the other *somethings*.

The Joy of TV Ads
Age 5

Just now, on one of Benny's kiddie channels, a commercial for a woman's hairbrush (no tangles, or something like that—not all that relevant for my head of sparse hair) came on.

Benny: I really think that Mommy should have this.

Matt: For real? Why?

B: Because her hairbrush can hurt her. Look, this one's smooth (close to verbatim).

M: I don't know. It's just a commercial.

B: It might be fake, but I think it works.

M: Should we get it for her as a present?

B: Yeah, maybe we should get it for Mother's Day.

M: Yeah, maybe.

B: (the commercial shows the various colors) Hey, it comes in red. Let's get it for her in red.

There's a fine line between being generous and being gullible.

Conservative Shopping
Age 5

We take Benny to the Thomas the Train ride (part of the Strasburg, PA railroad) and after the short ride, we visit one of the tents that serves as a gift shop.

As parents, we engage in what we also observe so many other moms and dads doing—trying to gently brainwash our kid into buying less expensive items.

"Oh, you have so many of those engines already—don't you think you'd enjoy this (cheap) shopping bag much more?" "Look at this pack of Thomas and Friends cookies. Hey, I think they're also very nutritious."

After some negotiating, we come away with not much damage: one of those cheap bags, and some (Thomas) Pez candy with a dispenser.

As we walk back to the car, Ruby notices some large pumpkins for sale and stops to take a look. Benny seizes the opportunity to enjoy a little role reversal.

"Mom, you don't have to buy everything you see, you know."

(None of the pumpkins go home with us, and Benny brings the Pez to dinner, and almost eats it for dessert.)

The tactics you deploy may come back to haunt you.

Bad Hosts
Age 5

Benny had a play date at a friend's—a girl named *Annie*. He was at their place for a few hours, and they even made him dinner. When I picked him up:

B: Dad, Annie's a bad host.

M: What do you mean?

B: She was a bad host.

M: How? They had you there for three hours. They gave you a change of clothes after you guys were playing with the hose, and they even made you dinner.

B: Yeah, but that was all Susan (her mom); Annie was still a bad host.

He's Learning...What?
Age 5

A couple weeks prior, Benny brought home a little worksheet about Venn Diagrams. This one was about bats and birds. There was a circle where you wrote properties of birds only, another for bats (only), and then an overlapping circle for things they have in common. I barely remembered this from school, and we made up another example or two that day, after which I forgot all about them again.

At the park, Benny is throwing stones into the creek, with his specialty of throwing two stones at once. I point out the separate ripples they make before merging together and crossing.

Benny assesses his work and says, "Look, a Venn Diagram."

When people are taught in fun ways that encourage imagination and play, they will remember.

Two out of Three Ain't Bad
Age 5

A little wisdom from my eternal (well, he's only 5, but I'm projecting) fountain of wisdom, Benny. The only background you need is that I am not much of a cook but am a little too proud of my scrambled eggs. Yes, they really are great!

Matt: So, Benny, do you want me to make you some of my world-famous eggs?

Benny: They're not famous.

M: What do you mean?

B: Things can't be famous; only people can.

M: No, not really. Books can be famous. So can movies like Star Wars. (We just watched it.)

B: Yes, but not everybody loves Star Wars.

M: Not everybody loves it, but almost everybody knows it—and—are you saying that not everybody loves my eggs?

B: Um-hmm

M: Why not?

B: Well, I like how they're made and how they smell. I just don't like how they taste.

(It's the little things.)

Critics will always find your weakest points.

Rake the Leaf and Put up the Decoration
Age 5

For his Religious School class, Benny has to write out (or bring in) some "mitzvah"—or report of a good deed that he said or did. We came up with the following sentence that I wrote out for him to copy: "I helped set up the Halloween decorations, and helped rake the leaves."

Benny: Dad, do I need to write the "s"?

Matt: Which one—in *leaves* or *decorations*?

B: In decorations.

M: Yes. Why not?

B: What if it's only one decoration?

M: Why would there only be one decoration? Can you give me an example?

B: On our front door, there's a decoration of a scarecrow.

Several
Age 5

Benny has been doing a little math with me in the mornings before school—using a book called "Time and Money." He's just starting with addition, and I try to, at times, see where he is with slightly more advanced concepts.

I ask him how many pages he wants to do today, and he replies, "Two."

Matt: Okay, you have 14 pages left in this book, so if you do two pages a day, how long will it take you to—

Benny: (He replies immediately, and I what I hear is...) Seven.

I'm astonished by the correct answer and the speed of his reply, as we've never done division and only kind of talked about 2 x 2 and other simple multiplication [things] a couple times):

M: Whoa, how did you get that so quickly?

B: What do you mean?

M: How did you know the answer was seven (days)?

B: I said "several".

M: What does "several" mean?

B: Just a little bit.

Oh...

Sometimes, moments of genius are missed, but at other times, they are mistakenly credited.

Still
Age 5

Benny has figured out a verbal strategy to which I have no successful counterattack. His key word is "still."

For example, I've been teaching him the basics of telling time—mostly from a book we picked up a month ago. On this one exercise, he has to tell if one time is earlier than another.

For example: *School starts at 1:00 (no am or pm yet). Dave arrives at 12:45. Is he early or late?*

Benny: He's late.

Matt: Are you sure that's the right answer?

B: Yes.

M: (We look at the clock). Actually, 12:45 comes before 1:00.

B: But, 12 is bigger than 1.

M: Yes, but, you have to go around the clock again, and 12 is actually before 1.

B: Still.

M: Still...what?

B: Still, being late is really like being early only being late is like being really, really, really early.

M: That's kind of true. But, this book is looking for less creative answers. And in this case, Dave is early for school.

B: Even so...

(He picked up "still" from somewhere else, but why did I teach him "even so?" Still, and even so, I love him more than these few words can convey.)

Trouble-ness
Age 5

I was 'quizzing' Benny about his "K" class, such as *Who is the tallest? Who is the noisiest/quietest, etc?*

And then:

Matt: Who is the funniest? (I expected him to nominate himself, but)

Benny: *Herb.*

M: What makes Herb the funniest?

B: He's just funny. But his funniness leads to trouble-ness.

Changing Benny?
Age 5

Benny is changing into a pair of warmup-type pants, and is getting confused as to the back and front. I point out the design.

Matt: See that design; that goes on the front.

Benny: That's not a design. It's just something to make the pants look fancier.

M: But, isn't that what a design is, um, designed to do?

B: Yes.

I think I *won* one. I'll stop this anecdote here.

Don't be a quitter, but if you do quit, do so while you're ahead.

Seat Belts
Age 5

Benny is talking to me about how he and three other kids (they're the only ones on his afternoon kindergarten bus) are really rowdy on the way to school.

Matt: You can't be too rowdy.

Benny: Why?

M: I mean, you have to be seated. You have to wear a seat belt.

B: (No reaction yet)

M: When I went to school, we didn't have seat belts on the bus.

B: YOU DIDN'T WEAR A SEAT BELT?!

M: No, they didn't have them.

B: Did you have seats?

If I Only Had a ...
Age 5

While watching *The Wizard of Oz*, Benny asks me what "courage" means.

Matt: It means not being afraid, or even if you are, not letting that fear stop you.

Benny: I don't have courage—

Before I can interject, Benny folds his fingers over like a monster with claws, moves them towards his face and then screams in horror.

Benny the Translator
Age 5

Ruby's on the speaker phone talking to a friend—in Mandarin. I ask Benny if he knows who Mom is talking to and he recognizes the voice.

Benny: Mommy just said [something like] "Go lai wai ni sha."

Matt: Great. What does that mean?

B: Come on over and play.

M: Really? Can you say that expression again slowly?

B: Come. on. over. and. Play.

He's so helpful.

Imprecise questions may lead to unsatisfying results.

The greatest gift we can offer our children—and ourselves—is our presence.

Thanks-stretching
Age 5

Benny had an in-class assignment to list some things that "I am thankful for..."

His list—and I write verbatim (it looks better in his handwriting):

wrld

mommy

cusins

daddy

hos

food

to

Matt: Nice list, Benny. What's the last one: "to?"

Benny: Oh, that was supposed to be "toy."

M: Okay...and the first one. Is it—?

B: Word.

M: You're thankful for "word" or "world?"

B: Both.

M: What's the one after "daddy?"

138

B: House.

M: What happened to the other vowels (He *is* just in kindergarten.)?

B: We weren't supposed to write them all. We were supposed to STRETCH them out.

M: But, how come you wrote out "mommy" and "daddy" correctly?

B: You didn't need any stretching.

Shiny Happy What?
Age 5

We see the word "shiny" in a book, so...

Matt: What does the word "shiny" mean?

Benny: Shiny means sparkly and pretty.

M: Good. Can you use "shiny" in a sentence?

B: Okay. Pennies are shiny like rubies are shiny.

M: Great. How about one more?

B: Why is your heiny so big and shiny?

Cut to two "men" erupting in laughter.

It's okay, and yes, even fun, to indulge your child's (and your own) silliness.

White Elephants
Age 5

We're looking for some items for a white elephant exchange, for the night's Toastmasters meeting. I ask Benny if he wants to donate this silly, colored caterpillar of his. It's soft, with a couple sections that squeak.

Benny: No, I want to keep that.

Matt: Why? You don't really use it anymore.

B: I have to save it for my own babies.

Months later, Benny and Ruby had the same discussion about his football-shaped toilet seat that he no longer needs.

It's a virtue to plan ahead. The key is to also do so with some flexibility.

Only Natural
Age 5

Benny, his big cousin Alex, and another friend built some kind of bird's nest the previous day. Alex goes to check on it and disappointed, says, "It's not there. Somebody kicked it away."

Benny's reaction: "Alex, as long as you try to get nature to come here, it will never come."

It's not always easy to attribute the source(s) of your children's wisdom.

Pair of Pants
Age 5

Tonight, Benny's reading from a (surprisingly complex) book-in-a-bag, and well...

Benny: "A little farther on, the little old lady stumbled into a pair of pants." Daddy, that doesn't make sense.

Matt: What doesn't make sense?

B: Why is it a *pair* of pants? It's only one.

M: Yes, but—there are two sections.

B: There are supposed to be two.

M: But each one is a "pant." Let me demonstrate. (I pull one of my legs out of my warm-up pants and try to walk around.) See, now I'm wearing "a pant."

B: That makes no sense.

M: Yeah, you're right.

Big is Small
Age 5

As part of Benny's homework assignment, he has to write the word "big" in a sentence. He only has a little room (two lines that go halfway across the page), given how big he still writes. Today's word is "ball".

I take a look: Benny has written "My big ball..."

Matt: What's the rest of your sentence?

Benny: My big ball is shaped like a circle.

M: Can you fit all that in?

B: My big ball is shaped like a circle and I want to play with it this afternoon.

Tripping Out
Age 5.5

Matt: I'm going to make a trip to CVS. Do you need anything?

Benny: That's not a trip.

M: Why not?

B: It's not long enough.

M: How about when you get to school on the bus. Is that a trip?

B: No.

M: To the bathroom?

B: No!

M: To New York?

B: Yes.

M: To China?

B: Yes.

M: To the miniature golf place?

B: No.

I couldn't *trip* him up.

Valentine's Day
Age 5.5

Ruby had accompanied Benny to his class Valentine's Day party. She tells me about something that happened in which Benny's reaction was a little surprising.

Matt (a little later on): Benny, I can't figure you out sometimes.

Benny: What do you mean?

M: You're still a mystery to me.

B: You're never gonna solve the mystery until you're old and grey.

I'm getting there. Trust me.

In between the precocious wisdom of youth and the sage wisdom of our elder years, there may be a lot of puzzling years.

An Important Question?
Age 5.5

Benny had heard that moths are attracted to lights (or flames) so, yesterday I searched for a little more information about it. From an article I read online, this seemed to be more myth than reality, as moths are nocturnal. But, I mentioned to him that I wasn't 100% sure about it.

So, today:

Benny: Dad, can we see God?

Matt: No, not really.

B: Why not?

M: HE's everywhere, including in our hearts, and our imagination.

B: I'd like to see him.

M: Why?

B: I'd ask him if moths are really attracted to lights.

When you believe in God, it's easy to believe that no problem is too big or too small.

Where's My Window?
Age 5.5

The three of us are riding in the car, and Ruby says that she can see a rainbow.

Ruby: Benny, take a look at the rainbow. It's beautiful.

Benny: I can't see it. But, I don't like rainbows, anyway.

Matt: Benny, you've always liked rainbows.

B: Is there a window on top of my head?

M: What do you mean?

B: How do you know what my brain is thinking if I don't have a window on top of my head?

As well as you may think you know your children (and what they enjoy), there are limits.

Birthday Card
Age 5.5

Benny is writing out a birthday card for a classmate who has a party tomorrow. After writing, "Dear *Ethan*,"...

Benny: Dad, I'm not sure what to say.

Matt: Just write a little something you want to say to him, or wish him.

B: *"Dear Ethan, I hope I'll have a good time at your birthday party."*

Everyone attending a party should have a good time!

3 Questions
Age 5.5

Being an analytical dad sometimes means seeing the brilliance of my son's casual comments, and other times wondering what's going through his mind. A few snippets from today:

I.

Benny: When you were young (100 or so questions a day start this way), did you watch *Family Guy*?

Matt: No, it wasn't around back then.

B: How do you *know*? (I get *this* one 10-20 times a day)

M: I just know; it wasn't around then.

B: So, you remember every single TV show that was on back then?

II.

Benny: Dad, when will it be tomorrow?

Matt: Tomorrow.

B: When is that?

M: After midnight tonight.

B: So tonight, when I go to sleep, will it be tomorrow?

M: Probably.

B: And when I wake up, will it be light out?

M: I hope so.

B: Good, I want to stay up till after midnight again.

III.

I told Benny that we need to do a birthday card for my niece/his cousin:

Benny: How old will she be?

Matt: 17. Wow, I can still remember when she was a baby?

B: How old was she when she was a baby?

M: How old do you think?

B: I don't know. One.

M: Well, at first, she wasn't even one until she had her first birthday.

B: Dad, do you remember me when I was zero?

The Other Side of the Street
Age 5.5

I've had a real tough time since yesterday's root canal, with a ton of throbbing and almost no sleep the last 12 hours. I was complaining a bit this morning, and well...

Benny: Dad, a root canal doesn't sound too bad.

M: I know, but—

B: It sounds like a street or something

(I'm thinking that the right side of my mouth is like 5th Avenue during rush hour.)

M: Maybe, *you'd* like to have a root canal then?

B: Why would I want my own street?

It's always easy to give away something of negative value.

Upstaged
Age 5.5

Benny doesn't always get in the last, or most precocious, word. He usually does— but not always, as this example will illustrate. Tonight, at a holiday service (for the Jewish holiday of Purim) a young girl sits next to Benny. After just a little prompting from his dad, he starts the introduction process.

Benny: Hi, I'm five-and-a-half

Anonymous Cutie: I'm four-and-a-quarter.

Regardless of whether the number is small or large, be proud of your years, and make every half (and even quarter) count.

Youthful Recollections
Age 5.5

Benny and Ruby are enjoying a deep conversation.

Benny: When you were young, was *Cartoon Network* around?

Ruby: No, not yet.

B: Mommy, almost everything came out when I was young, cause I'm still young.

Theory of Age Relativity
Age 5.5

The Theory of Age Relativity with Benny just now: Feel free to take notes.

David, the younger brother of his good friend, turns four on April 30.

Benny: So, he'll be one month older than me?

Matt: No, you're older than he is. He's only 3 now, and you're 5.

B: But, his birthday comes before mine.

M: Yes, but your birthday comes before mine. Does that make you older than me?

B: No!

(pause)

B: Hey Dad, when I get to be your age, I'll be older than you.

M: How does that work? Will I stop having birthdays?

B: (changing his tack) Dad, when I'm a grown-up, you'll be really old.

M: Thanks for the reminder.

As previously said, regardless of whether the number is small or large, be proud of your years, and make every year (and day) meaningful!

Early Bird
Age 5.5

Just after 6 am on a lazy "Spring Break" morning, Benny comes into our room

Benny: Mommy. Listen!

Ruby (still in a sleep-induced fog): Huh?

B: The birds are singing.

R: So?

B: That means it's morning. Time to get up.

Matt: Benny, you went to bed after midnight. You need to get another few hours of sleep.

B: Why do you always have to judge time, Dad?

Wardrobe Consultant
Age 5.5

I don't need to get dressed up too often, but need to this morning. I ask Ruby (and Benny, by extension) which of two shirts (both in packages, unopened) I should wear: the white one, or the tan-colored one.

Benny's advice? "That one (white) looks like a doctor's shirt, and that one (tan/brown) looks like a park ranger."

Both were kind of wrinkled, so I went with Option 3.

Dress respectfully, but keep your own identity in the process.

Happy Earth Day
Age 5.5

Last night, Ruby was watching Benny brush his teeth before taking a bath. He suddenly turns off the faucet and proclaims:

Benny: Look Mommy, I'm saving the planet.

(A couple moments later)

B: I'm not going to take any more baths.

(Sounds ominous)

I'm gonna take a shower every day.

Police Rock
Age 5.5

Benny: When I grow up, my job will be a police, and also a singer with a band.

Matt: What will the name of your rock band be?

B: *The Thes*

M: *The The's*? That reminds me. In college, my senior year, our intramural basketball team was named "The." Are you sure your band's name will be like this?

B: Well, maybe we'll have a name like *The Flying Dragons*, but I don't know what I'll call it when I'm a grownup. (more animated now) How am I supposed to know what I'm going to think of when I'm a grown-up? Dad, did you know what grown-up life would be like when you were a kid?

Be patient with those around you, including yourself.

A "Boll" of What?
Age 5.5

As the school year nears its conclusion, Benny has been sent home from school (kindergarten) with all kinds of work from earlier this year. For this one project, apparently, he had to fill in the blank to "If I could fly like a butterfly..."

Says my boy "...I would go in a boll [sic.] of snacks. I like snacks."

Hut, Hut
Almost 6

Benny and I picked up a takeout pizza a little while ago from a Pizza Hut.

Benny: Da-ad, this place is so small.

Matt: Yeah, it's just for carry-out. (We usually eat in at another [better?} place.

B: There aren't any tables or silverware—anything. Why?

M: Yes, it's just a takeout place.

B: Why's it so small?

M: Because it's just—

B: I know. Because it's a hut, and a hut's a small house.

Truth in advertising goes a long way.

Relief Map?
Almost 6

We're in a CVS Pharmacy, and they have a sign with a map of the US, and the various states that have CVS stores highlighted with red dots.

Benny sees it first and calls out to me: "Dad, why does the world have chicken pox?"

It's never too early to be concerned with the welfare of all those around you.

Employment Advice
Almost 6

Ruby's sister, Linda, calls us from the airport. She's on the way to China on business, with her son, Alex (Benny's cousin) staying with us for several weeks.

Benny comes on the phone and says: Hi, Yimama (Chinese word for maternal aunt). Have a good time at work. Don't get fired!

The Ferris Wheel
Almost 6

Here's a Benny-ism that Ruby was a part of—it requires just a little explanation, but it blew my mind when I heard about it. We went to a carnival on Saturday night with another family. Benny has known their oldest daughter (call her ("Elena") since she was a baby. She's almost 5; he's almost 6.

Benny's big cousin, Alex (he's 9-and-a-half, but bigger than many 11-year-olds) is with us for a month or so, and also went to the carnival. Last night, they were talking in the bathroom.

Benny: Alex, when you went on the Ferris wheel with Elena, did you find yourself falling in love with her?

Alex (shocked): What?! She's not even 5, and I'm 9. She's not even half as old as me.

B: So?

Later, Ruby asked Benny about it, and he explained...

B: Well, the Ferris wheel can be very romantic.

(Apparently) Romance, like reality and beauty, is in the eye(s) of the beholder.

Choosing the Better Listener
Almost 6

I'm getting the feeling that I could be frustrating to live with at times. But it is so much fun.

Benny: (starting to tell a story) Dad, do you remember yesterday—

M: (interrupting) No, I don't think I do.

B: Do you remember yesterday—

M: (interrupting again) I think I do. When was yesterday?

B: (silent)

M: Oh yeah, you mean the day before today?

B: Dad, do you remember yesterday when Zachary sent Mom a text—

M: Why would he send Mom a test? Is she in school?

B: Mom, do you remember when Zach sent you a text?

There's always someone willing to listen to you if you're patient enough.

That's Where He Gets It
Age 6

A doubleheader of Benny-isms broke out today.

I.

I can't remember what we were discussing, but he said something (teasing me in some way) that I had to challenge in a juvenile way.

Matt: Benny, I'm gonna have to call the Fire Department; I think your pants are on fire.

Benny: You mean like, Liar, liar, pants on fire / put your heiny in the tire?

M: Something like that.

• • •

II.

B: Daddy, do you like to barbecue?

M: Not really.

B: Why?

M: I don't know, but Mommy does it so well. (a confession)

B: But all boys like to barbecue.

M: How do you know that? Did you read that somewhere?

B: (big smile as he points to his brain): Yep. It's in my Invisible Book of Everything.

It's all About Timing
Age 6

I told Benny that we were invited to watch the Eagles game at a friend's house (who he knows), which inspired this exchange.

Benny: So, are we the only people there?

Matt: No, another friend or two will be there, plus *Parker* and his wife. Well, his fiancé, *Cheryl*.

B: They're not married yet?

M: No, but they're engaged.

B: Oh, have they had all their dates already?

A Major *Miner*
Age 6

Benny is doing wonderfully in his early first-grade writing assignments, even if his spelling is sometimes creative. On this particular assignment, his drawing was also wonderful, but I'll leave that detail to your imagination.

The theme of the essay was When I Grow Up...; his teacher rewarded him with a "Great Writing" comment.

I want too be a m-(end of line)

inere becus I mite get 1000 dollers or 100 dollers that is why I like mines. My second reason why I like mineres is becus I can be on my frens team. That is why I want too be a minere. I am so exidide too be a minere.

Encourage your children to dream big and let their creativity flourish.

Cutting Up
Age 6

It's *tough* living with a little wordsmith with a great sense of humor. We're preparing for a small Halloween party later that night, and I ask Ruby if I should pick up a pumpkin pie or two. My offer is shot down.

Matt: Okay. Actually, I need to cut down on junk food.

Benny: I need to cut *up* on junk food.

M: What are you going to cut up on?

B: I'll cut up on more cookies, do-dos (what we call doughnuts), cakes and pies.

Three-Finger Discount?
Age 6

I overheard this during Benny's play date here with his friend *Peter*. This took place while I was watching an intense Eagles (NFL) game.

Peter: Do you know the names of your fingers?

Benny: Yes, I've named them.

P: Really? What are their names?

B: This one's Dave, this is Jay, and that's Kai.

Fingers should only be given one-syllable names. (Please don't ask me why.)

Outward Silence
Age 6

I was reminding Benny that I had to take him with me to a meeting (in this case, a Toastmasters speech contest) tonight, so I suggested he bring a new book with him.

Matt: So, you can bring this, and what else can you do quietly?

Benny: I can bring my Legos.

(Apparently, I shot him an incredulous look.)

B: What? I can talk in my brain.

(Another look, but this time while half-laughing.)

B: I can. I do this all the time, you know.

I'll See Your 65 Mil and...
Age 6

The three of us returned quite late from a good friend of Ruby's surprise party a few minutes before and—from the bathroom—Benny had a burning question for me.

B: Daddy, when did the dinosaurs become extinct?

M: I don't know; about 65 million years ago.

B: It can't be.

M: Why?

B: Because it's almost New Year's, and—

M: So, what's your point (I just wanted him to spell it out.)

B: Because you have to add another year now.

Whose Business?
Age 6

This conversation ensued about a half-hour after I brought Benny home from a play date.

Benny: Dad, why did you pick me up early tonight?

Matt: I didn't. I said I would come between 6:45 and 7, and came about five minutes to 7.

B: Oh...

M: Hey Benny, I saw *Pete's* older brother, but was his sister home?

B: I don't know.

M: I guess they're both busy. They both do sports and other—

B: Dad, why are you concerned with other people's business?

(I start to laugh and then...)

B: Dad, that's not a Benny-ism, is it?

M: Hmm...It might be.

Every promise, big and small alike, is worth keeping.

Best of Both Worlds
Age 6

Benny's writing out holiday cards accompanying little presents to his first-grade teacher and his bus driver. He did a nice job, and I noticed that he wrote "From Benny" to his teacher and "Love, Benny" to his bus driver. I expressed surprise, so he changed the one to his teacher as "From the love of Benny."

Upsmanship
Age 6

Ruby and I pick up a used game (Upwords, which I've never played before) and Benny and I are playing around with it. I spell out the word d-e-a-f, and ask Benny if he knows what the word means.

Benny: Does it mean 'death', for someone who has a lazy "th"?

Wow! As is often the case, I don't know where he comes up with this shtik.

Dark (Environmental) Secrets
Age 6

We were watching some video on YouTube (age appropriate, of course) and he asked me to look up "Five Dark Secrets of an Apple." I'm not sure how he'd heard of that, but I clicked on it, and it was about the company, and not the fruit.

He was a little surprised/disappointed, and then he suddenly—with no prompting—said, and I quote, as closely as I can:

"The Five Dark Secrets of Benny:

1. He's nice.

2. He has toys.

3. He eats.

4. He did what Nik Wallenda did on the tightrope thingy in Chicago.

and

#5. He likes to take care of the earth."

There is a lot that I still don't understand about Benny, but I can vouch for all of these, with the probable exception of #4.

Be present, be loving, and be involved with your children, but don't be upset when you don't know everything.

Pet Peeves of a Pre-School Daddy

...in which the author (sort of) learns how to
just chill out and enjoy the ride.

Even in those very early years of fatherhood, seeing one's son grow up comes with some mixed feelings. I had blogged the following during the first week of Benny's first year (of two) in pre-school. Since then, I think I have learned to just "chill" and enjoy the ride. Most of the time.

. . .

I can't say that it came suddenly, but when I take a step back, it seems just a little odd that we're taking our three-year-old son, Benny, to school every day. Yes, it took me a long time to enter fatherhood and Benny's been jabbering for months and months about going to school. This didn't exactly sneak up on us.

And it is only pre-school, a two-and-a-half hour glorified play time that won't determine whether he goes to Harvard at age 15 or still struggles with his GED at age 33. Still, my wife Ruby and I want Benny to get off to a good start. Has he?

Maybe, I'm seeking some unattainable picture of perfection here, but I'm just not sure.

Yes, he still loves school after his first three days, and there's been no separation anxiety on his end. He goes right into the classroom and gives us almost nonchalant, teenager-like goodbyes when he enters Room 102. From my perspective, I guess this beats the heck out of the ten-minute wail, popularized by a couple of his classmates.

When we pick him up, he's happy to see us, if not desperate to break out of Alcatraz. He even shares a happy detail or two about his day with us. "That little boy started crying, Mama,

Mama until his Mommy came." "We read Clifford—the Big Red Dog."

So, why am I complaining? Is it my self-appointed mission in life to ferret out the seedy underbelly of township pre-schools or to find the cloud that holds the silver? Or do mixed feelings just kind of find me—in all avenues of life?

Okay, his teacher seems nice enough, and my quick, baseball-like scouting report on her would be: Positive, fairly upbeat if not overly so...attractive, if not distractingly so...hits with occasional power.

Ms. P was nice enough in our pre-class, pre-school meeting a couple days before the official Day One. Ruby, Benny and I had a 20-minute get-to-know-her-and-the-classroom meeting. Benny was very reserved that day, and Ms. P didn't say a whole lot. I dragged some answers out of her. Our little guy felt at home, even if he exhibited a quieter version of his usual self, and all was good.

Last Friday afternoon, the experience with Ms. P was just a little different. Let me explain.

When I asked her how Benny was doing, she responded with a lukewarm, "Okay."

Just okay?

I was fishing in the compliment pond, hoping it would be stocked. It wasn't.

"Not bad."

Gee, I hardly said anything, and my son's status was downgraded. If this were a weather report, the partly cloudy day was now steady rain, but no ruinous hail. I should've stopped fishing in this pond, but I did bring my rod, if very poor bait. Or maybe, my bait was only attractive to piranhas.

Oh, has Benny been following directions?

"Well, it's only been two days," assured Ms. P.

Hold on there, Ms. P, what do you mean, "It's only been two days?"

What kind of trouble and destruction can our rather perfect, brilliant and sweet, sensitive 37 month-old have caused in just five hours of classroom time? He's always come home in a good mood, with unsoiled pants and a half-eaten snack. Room 102 always seems to be standing at the end of the day. What happened?

I pondered this and more, and I wondered if Ms. P was trying not to get our hopes up too high, or if she (thought she) was just being nice. Now, I admit that I am one to jump to conclusions and be rather "un-chill" (pronounced tight-assed) when it comes to Benny. But, what the heck?

He doesn't always listen to us, and I guess that we don't demand that he does so all the time. And when we play silly games like Diggity Dog (don't look at me like that: you've all played that board game) we do play by official Benny rules. Still, I'm sure that he listens most of the time, and plays pretty well with others. He almost always does so at the playground.

And even if he can be a little stubborn, he's just so darned entertaining as he goes about it. He's long ago surpassed cute, even if he hasn't totally outgrown cute and adorable. What and who has Ms P been observing?

And if they challenge him a little, I'm sure he'll be reading every book in their little classroom library independently by Thanksgiving.

And another thing: How come he never comes home with any art work or anything educational in his knapsack? Yes, we did get the reminder to pay our monthly tuition, and the other notice asking for classroom donations. We also got the note that the school and classroom was thrilled to be part of Scholastic Publishing's free books program; all we had to do to participate was to pick out books and pay for them.

Huh? I asked that question, too.

What's going on here? And don't they realize how high our property taxes are?! I tried to stop myself from going postal over a simple "not bad" and "it's only been two days." It's hard to do so once I get my momentum going. I can generally control my actions and my spoken words; it's just the other stuff that I write and think about. Sometimes the writing comes before the thoughts, sometimes they occur simultaneously.

A thought hit me: Was I becoming a terrible, pushy parent in the making—the kind of creature I've always reviled. Let's see: There was Joan Crawford, Michael Jackson's dad and a million of other overzealous parents. Oy! Not me.

But it is a tough transition for me to hear anything remotely negative about my son. And, we've been spoiled with a kid who, objectively, women (and even some grown men) gravitate to and swoon over. But at some point, his every thought, belch and breaking of wind will go from the coolest thing ever to a terrible annoyance. Is he already in this uncharted territory, and how will all of us adjust to these new rules?

The weekend came and went quickly, and on Day 3, I dropped Benny off and Ruby picked him up. I did not want to be tempted to fish in Ms P's pond at the end of the day. I was happy to notice that Benny's knapsack contained a new art project. Ah, some tangible evidence of education!

Benny proudly—and with his customary sense of humor—explained the school bus of which he (at least assisted in) glued little black triangles for windows, the front door, and, and, some other avant-garde pattern that defied description. An observation here. He's already a better visual artist than his Dad. If I had to pass Art 101 to graduate high school, I may have been the one going for my GED at age 33.

With just a little more perspective and time, I took Benny to school a couple hours ago for Day Four. Although it was a beautiful day, I started thinking about how old the school building looked. Not quite outdated, but certainly not modern. Not about to fall apart, but not quite venerable or stately.

I noticed the cornerstone for the first time. 1959—yes, the very year I was born.

Was the building trying to tell me something?

A Treasury of 100 Life Lessons

1. Never celebrate your triumphs prematurely. (pg.2)

2. You may suspect that your son or daughter is smarter than you. Don't worry; your suspicion is probably on solid ground. (pg. 4)

3. One person's reassurance is (sometimes) another's cause for concern. (pg.5)

4. Our children are not trained seals: Don't expect them to perform on command. (pg.6)

5. When correcting others, always be specific. (pg.8)

6. Your children pay attention to everything you say, do and watch. (pg.9)

7. The best prizes are often the ones we don't actively pursue. (Or, if you prefer: The best prizes are often surprises.) (pg.11)

8. Often, the best solutions are close at hand, and sometimes right on our hands and clothing. (pg.12)

9. We don't all share the same preferences. (pg.13)

10. Not all of us relax in the same way. (pg. 14)

11. Music (even Madonna, and The Chipmunks) uniquely brings people together. (pg.15)

12. Always encourage your kids (and yourself) to embrace new challenges. (pg.16)

13. As "they" say, humor is often the best medicine. (pg.17)

14. If you have to surrender, do so on your own terms. (pg.19)

15. Use imagination and persistence to solve problems. (pg.20)

16. The answer is often better than the question. So, keep asking questions. (pg.22)

17. Don't be afraid to share your special talents with the world. (pg.23)

18. We sometimes relate to the same people in slightly different ways. (pg.24)

19. Tangents are often more interesting than the main route. (pg.25)

20. It is often better to concede a point than to argue it. (pg.26)

21. One is never too old to learn, or too young to teach. (pg.27)

22. Stay close to those you love (and try to stay out of trouble.) (pg.28)

23. When you issue a challenge to someone, don't be surprised when the challenge is met. (pg.29)

24. When it comes to gardens and life, itself, always dwell on the bright side. (pg.30)

25. It's important to know your place(s). (pg.31)

26. What's amusing to you may not be amusing to others. (pg.32)

27. It's not easy to distract a hungry carnivore, yet it may be well worth the effort. (pg.34)

28. Always be truthful, and consistent. (pg. 35)

29. It's okay to be left speechless, at times. (pg. 36)

30. Give your children the tools to succeed, and hope that they use them as you intended. (pg. 37)

31. Age is a relative matter. (pg. 38)

32. Don't be in a hurry to reach every destination. (pg. 39)

33. It's awesome to share with others, and to return what you've borrowed in a timely manner. (pg. 40)

34. They tell us that we, as parents, are supposed to have all the answers. Who are they, and what do they know that we don't? (pg.43)

35. Play with others in a way that they will want to play with you again. (pg. 44)

36. Don't wait for others to introduce themselves first. (pg. 45)

37. There's an art to skillfully deflecting tough questions. (pg. 47)

38. Nurture your inner child: Don't neglect the importance of playing, eating and sleeping enough! (pg. 49)

39. Don't be bound by everyone else's expectations of time. (pg. 51)

40. Engage your kids in conversation. You may even be rewarded with a whale of a story. (pg. 56)

41. Communicate clearly, so you don't set false expectations. (pg. 57)

42. Don't let your plans get washed away too soon. (pg. 58)

43. Meals are more enjoyable when shared with those we love. At the same time, it is just sustenance, right? (pg. 61)

44. The best told stories of mice and men sometimes change over the years. (pg. 64)

45. If you want someone to agree with you, tell them what you think they want to hear. (pg. 65)

46. A sweet tooth and an impatient nature can lead to unhealthy results. (pg. 67)

47. We all need to feel like a superhero at times. How do we achieve that status? It all starts with love and kindness. (pg. 70)

48. When you make a good choice, be proud of it. (pg. 71)

49. Self-belief is the first step toward achieving something great. (pg. 73)

50. If you err, err on the side of too much honesty. (pg. 75)

51. We learn compassion when we wear other people's shoes. (pg. 77)

52. Use your power of free speech to speak well of others. (pg. 80)

53. Make every effort to serve your guests (even the uninvited ones) what they like to eat. (pg. 82)

54. The importance of taking turns—socially and historically—cannot be overstated. (pg. 84)

55. A determined mind will always find a way to his destination. (pg. 85)

56. Learning isn't always conveyed from teacher to student or from parent to child. Learning happens in all directions, both formally and informally, by design and accident alike. (pg. 89)

57. Sometimes, as parents, we'll be (seemingly) relegated to second banana status behind TV, movie and book characters. Don't worry; it's only temporary. (pg. 80)

58. Show your kids the way, and if they outdo you, so much the better. (pg. 91)

59. Not everyone can be the best at everything, right? (pg. 94)

60. Hiding seldom solves your problems—especially if your hiding place is under a rhino's butt. Think about it...if you wish. (pg. 96)

61. When conversing with someone that has a fertile mind, it's okay to give him the last word. (pg. 97)

62. Patience is a virtue, but impatience usually begets more impatience. (pg. 99)

63. The irrelevance of mythology is simply a myth. (pg. 100)

64. In games, as in life in general, there are official rules and self-made rules of convenience. Both have their place. (pg. 102)

65. Always respect the dignity of those around you—regardless of age or any other factor. (pg. 103)

66. It's always good to know what you don't know. Now, use that knowledge as a springboard to learn more. (pg. 106)

67. It's okay to cry sometimes. Really. By the same token, don't accuse someone of crying when they haven't. (pg. 107)

68. As a rule, honesty is always best, but too much honesty can devalue your own act of generosity. (pg. 108)

69. Just one little piece of evidence can invalidate an otherwise strong argument. (pg. 110)

70. Some wonderful things just have to be experienced. (pg. 114)

71. Reality, like beauty, is sometimes in the eye(s) of the beholder. (pg. 115)

72. The best way to learn (and to teach) is to involve all the senses. (pg. 117)

73. There's a fine line between being generous and being gullible. (pg. 119)

74. The tactics you deploy may come back to haunt you. 9pg. 121)

75. When people are taught in fun ways that encourage imagination and play, they will remember. (pg. 123)

76. Critics will always find your weakest points. (pg. 125)

77. Sometimes, moments of genius are missed, but at other times, they are mistakenly credited. (pg. 128)

78. Don't be a quitter, but if you do quit, do so while you're ahead. (pg. 132)

79. Imprecise questions may lead to unsatisfying results. (pg. 135)

80. The greatest gift we can offer our children—and ourselves—is our presence. (pg. 137)

81. It's okay—and yes, even fun— to indulge your child's (and your own) silliness. (pg. 139)

82. It's a virtue to plan ahead. The key is to also do so with some flexibility. (pg. 141)

83. It's not always easy to attribute the source(s) of your children's wisdom. (pg. 142)

84. In between the precocious wisdom of youth and the sage wisdom of our elder years, there may be a lot of puzzling years. (pg. 146)

85. When you believe in God, its easy to believe that no problem is too big or too small. (pg. 147)

86. As well as you may think you know your children (and what they enjoy), there are limits. (pg. 148)

87. Everyone attending a party should have a good time! (pg. 149)

88. It's always easy to give away something of negative value. (pg. 152)

89. Regardless of whether the number is small or large, be proud of your years, and make every half (and even quarter) count. (pg. 153)

90. As previously said, regardless of whether the number is small or large, be proud of your years, and make every year (and day) meaningful! (pg. 156)

91. Dress respectfully, but keep your own identity in the process. (pg. 158)

92. Be patient with those around you, including yourself. (pg. 160)

93. Truth in advertising goes a long way. (pg. 162)

94. It's never too early to be concerned with the welfare of all those around you. (pg. 163)

95. (Apparently) Romance, like reality and beauty, is in the eye(s) of the beholder. (pg. 165)

96. There's always someone willing to listen to you if you're patient enough. (pg. 166)

97. Encourage your children to dream big and let their creativity flourish. (pg. 170)

98. Fingers should only be given one-syllable names. (Please don't ask me why.) (pg. 172)

99. Every promise, big and small alike, is worth keeping. (pg. 175)

100. Be present, be loving, and be involved with your children, but don't be upset when you don't know everything. (pg. 179)

A Final Word

Although this formal, *informal* collection of Benny-isms has drawn to a close, the stories and anecdotes will (without a shadow of a doubt) continue as he continues to grow, and I continue to try to catch up with him.

Speaking of which, here's just one more for you. For 2015, Benny really wanted to buy New Year's presents for me and Ruby, his cousin Alex and Aunt Linda (who were visiting us) and one of his very close friends who had been away for a couple weeks. Ruby withdrew some money from his piggy bank, and on the way to the roller skating rink, we stopped at one of the dollar stores.

Benny was excited to deliver a couple artificial roses to Ruby, and exclaimed, "They're fake, Mommy, so they'll last forever!"

Ironically, some of these little nothing/everything moments will last forever precisely because they are so genuine.

I hope that this book has inspired you to not only laugh, smile and think about some of your own stories, but to also consider one or two of the life lessons inspired by Benny on these pages. If you would like to share any of your own stories with me— especially if they were inspired by *Hot Ice Cream*—I would love to read all about them.

And so will Benny, I'm sure.

You may pass them, along with any comments or requests, to me via matt@tipofthegoldberg.com.

Thank you. I look forward to seeing or hearing from you soon.

About the Author

Matt Goldberg is an inspirational humorist who is passionate about inspiring others to achieve more while laughing, smiling and learning just a little bit more. As a writer and a speaker, his goal is to communicate with hilarity and clarity. That is a rarity.

Matt resides in Cherry Hill, NJ, a suburb of Philadelphia, and is an author, custom writer and editor, all-around speaker, and presentations coach. Interests include the above, plus a variety of sports (to play, watch, and write about), the arts, education, and volunteer activities. Most of all, he values his time and those little nothing/everything moments with his wife (Ruby) and son (Benny).

He has previously authored five other books, and he currently writes about a variety of topics via the "Goldblog" on his site, www.tipofthegoldberg.com. His previously published book titles are:

A Snowball's Chance: Philly Fires Back Against the National

Media

All That Twitters is Not Goldberg

Wordapodia, Volume One

Mixed Emotions: Poetry for the Open-Minded

So So Wisdom: the Misplaced Teachings of So So Gai

All requests (for speaking engagements, coaching, book events, writing, editing and more) can be sent via matt@tipofthegoldberg.com.

www.ingramcontent.com/pod-product-compliance
Lightning Source LLC
LaVergne TN
LVHW051509080426
835509LV00017B/1989